THE SUCCESSION PRINCIPLE

The Succession Principle

How Leaders Make Leaders

DAVID L. McKENNA

foreword by
GAYLE D. BEEBE

CASCADE *Books* · Eugene, Oregon

THE SUCCESSION PRINCIPLE
How Leaders Make Leaders

Cascade Books
An Imprint of Wipf and Stock Publishers
199 W. 8th Ave., Suite 3
Eugene, OR 97401

www.wipfandstock.com

ISBN 13: 978-1-4982-0479-8

Cataloging-in-Publication data:

McKenna, David L., 1929–.

The succession principle : how leaders make leaders / David L. McKenna.

xii + 132 p.; 23 cm—Includes bibliographical references.

ISBN 13: 978-1-4982-0479-8

1. Leadership. 2. Leadership—Religious aspects—Christianity. 3. Bible. John—Criticism, interpretation, etc. I. Title.

BV652.1 .M3420 2015

Manufactured in the USA.

DEDICATED

to the

Students

in the

2015 Inaugural Class

of the

David and Janet McKenna
School of Education

at

Immanuel University,

Hyderabad, India

Contents

Foreword

"Now when David had served the purposes of God
in his own generation he 'rested.'"

—ACTS 13:36

I FIRST MET DAVID McKenna when we were both working in theological education. He was just finishing his distinguished career, while I was just beginning mine. I had always admired him and later accepted a call to the presidency at Spring Arbor University when he served as board chair. He combined a remarkable gift for leadership and administration with a brilliant mind, a relentless and dedicated spirit, and an uncanny ability to perceive trends and movements ahead of their time.

The challenge of succession is just such a trend. Leadership guru Jim Collins writes that the greatest leaders, the Level 5 leaders, combine personal humility with fierce resolve in accomplishing the greatest outcomes for their organizations. This always involves setting the stage for your successor's success. If your legacy is to live on, it must be embedded in an organization that will outlive you—and not just outlive you, but flourish after you finish as an indirect indicator of the contribution you made there.

Peter Drucker first identified and amplified the fact that the rise of the leader was tied directly to the rise of the complex organization in the twentieth century. Prior to 1900, very few companies or organizations employed more than a few hundred people. But that changed dramatically as organizations developed throughout the century. Having focused so completely on what makes an effective executive, Drucker overlooked commenting on what happens when you're gone.

David's own experience and accent on succession provides so much help here. Watching senior executives transition offers one of the great tests of character. Some do it well; many do it poorly. David helps us understand why. His exegesis of John 17 and the High Priestly Prayer provides the backdrop for the nuances we all face as we accept responsibility, initiate leadership, and strive to serve the purposes of God completely.

McKenna's incisive mind captures the dynamic interplay between personal motivation and corporate success. Effective leaders contribute to defining and advancing the mission and legacy of their organizations. They articulate vision, define goals, and pursue strategic priorities that make an enduring contribution. They create cultures that are life-giving and sustainable. They offer shared understandings and clear priorities. They address attitudes, behaviors, and conduct that detract from core purposes in order to ensure that every individual contributes to the greater good. But ultimately, having done all this work, a leader leaves a legacy tied to the health and vitality of the organization he or she led.

This eye on what happens after we are gone is so often neglected, if acknowledged at all. Dr. McKenna amplifies here that our responsibility as leaders includes planning our departures in such a way that we cast no shadow over our successors. He helps us find in the person and work of Jesus a capacity to recognize our contribution and then let go. Ultimately, he helps us recognize that our greatest legacy is to leave a place better than we found it: better resourced, better focused, and better aligned to guarantee momentum that can launch the leadership of those who follow us.

The epigraph above suggests the longing we all have to do the work God has placed us on earth to do and then let go. We want the joy that comes with accomplishment and the contentment that comes in knowing our contribution made a difference in the kingdom of God. Like King David of old, we want to rest with God and hear those blessed words, "Well done, O good and faithful servant." In the conclusion of our work, we find the meaning of our whole contribution.

Finally, David McKenna's own legacy is not only that he sees clearly, writes beautifully, and plans well, but that he contributed to the lives of so many of us in ways that will outlive him. I join the great cloud of witnesses who have been touched by his life, inspired by his leadership, and motivated by his legacy. Enjoy yet another source of his enduring contribution.

—Dr. Gayle D. Beebe, President, Westmont College

Introducing

THE SUCCESSION PRINCIPLE:

What we bring to our leadership is *important*;

What we do in our leadership is *more important*:

What we leave from our leadership is *most important of all.*

PROLOGUE

From Success to Succession

THIRTEEN YEARS AFTER RETIRING from the presidency at Asbury Theological Seminary, my wife, Janet, and I returned for graduation to receive an honorary degree. Before the commencement service I decided to do a proprietary check on the chapel that bears both of our names. Entering the lobby, I saw a graduate in cap and gown posing for a photograph in front of the oil painting of Janet and me. As I walked by she asked if I would take a picture of her with her family. I said "Of course" and aimed the camera to make sure that our faces in the oil painting provided the background for the shot. Then, with a bit of jest, I stepped in front of my own portrait, struck the same pose, and asked, "Do you see any resemblance?" They smiled and walked away. I was aghast! Either the painting was so bad or I had changed so much that they didn't even recognize me! So much for the fickle finger of fame.

This story adds another chapter to my unwritten book, *Humility and How I Achieved It*. Imagine walking into McKenna Hall at Seattle Pacific University, where our oldest son was teaching. When I introduced myself as David McKenna and inquired about the location of Dr. Douglas McKenna's office, the receptionist asked, "How do you spell that name?" Another time we arrived late in the evening for a campus speaking engagement and had to check through security in order to get the key to our room. The security guard at the desk was a former student whom I recognized by name and he, in turn, greeted me as "Dr. McKenna." Then, searching through the room reservations, he looked up and said, "May I see your I. D.?" So much for name recognition.

After nursing the bruises of an exaggerated ego, I began to rethink the whole idea of legacy in Christian leadership. Every Christian leader I know has an eye out for legacy. If we are honest we all want our name on a building, our portrait on a wall, and our place in the history books. Some of us are so obsessed with this thought that we work feverishly to assure life after leadership. One departing leader had his office duplicated in every detail and placed in a prominent place for all to see; another left several hundred boxes of everything he had written; and yet another offered a glass case collection displaying every memento from ribbons and certificates to trophies and photographs. From statues in the park to mottoes on the wall and vanity plates on the bumper, our Nixonian obsession with legacy lives on.

Others of us may disclaim such obvious attempts to assure our place in history but secretly check to make sure that we are recognized by name at public events and rewarded when credits are given. I confess that I have three manila envelopes in my desk drawer labeled "Publication," "Correspondence," and "Family." They are categories of items saved as additions to the McKenna Papers in the archives at Asbury Theological Seminary. Also, if you visit our condo I will casually show you framed pictures of buildings bearing our names at the institutions where we served, and in my study I hope that you notice the shelf of the books I wrote along with the framed citations for academic, religious, and community awards.

Am I alone or am I confessing for all of us? Are our egos so delicate that we feel slighted unless we continue to be remembered, recognized, and rewarded with honors front and center? Or, have our institutional cultures become so contaminated by a momentary mind-set that gratitude for leadership is limited to those who can answer the question, "What have you done for me lately?" While both of these factors play into the equation, they are not the cause of the problem. To have our leadership defined by names and numbers, fame and fortune, recognition and rewards is a show of self-interest. A legacy that reads like a scorecard of achievements is a secular giveaway of the very expectations by which a Christian leader is initially chosen and under which he or she serves.

Is it possible that we have again become victims of the success syndrome that dominates our culture? The symptoms are obvious: public image, tangible achievements, measurable goals, competitive wins, and visible awards. Of course, the acme of success is instant celebrity status based upon name, fame, and fortune. Like meteors in the sky, evangelical stars flash into view, create a temporary sensation, and then fade from sight because of the brilliance of a new star. The pop culture created by the media, both secular and Christian, goes hand in hand with the success syndrome.

Why are Christian leaders vulnerable to these counter-Christian influences? I remember the often-told story of the ship captain who was approached by a drug smuggler with an offer to become rich by secreting drugs in his cargo. Each time the captain said "No," the smuggler upped the ante until the amount was exorbitant. At that moment, the captain ordered, "Get off my boat. You are getting too close to my price." Perhaps this is our problem. When it comes to being seen as successful in the eyes of the world or enjoying celebrity status, the tempter has found our price.

It is time to rethink the meaning of legacy for Christian leaders. The starting point is to shift from our aspirations for success to our responsibilities for succession. To take this view of leadership is to invite a revolution. It is to make our successor more important than our success and what we give more important than what we get. Are we ready for the change?

1

Succession Revisited

SUCCESSION IS A TERM in transition. In ancient history "succession" meant the heritage of monarchy with the divine right of kings. Persons who were born of royal parents took their place in the line of succession to the throne. Without merit, they inherited the absolute power of a king or queen over all their subjects with accountability to God alone. The divine right of kings is long gone, but royal succession by birth continues. Princes and princesses still take their place in line for ascension to the throne where they are empowered with the authority to rule over a paper kingdom and given the task of trying to make meaning out of doing nothing.

In the world of business, succession also has a special meaning. Small family businesses in particular have a line of succession, as children and grandchildren inherit ownership from parents and grandparents. A newspaper ad in Seattle features four generations of a family in the furniture business sitting on a sofa. In succession, the picture shows the ninety-year-old grandfather, a seventy-year-old son, a forty-year-old grandson, and an eighteen-month-old great-grandson bouncing on his father's knee. The ad needs no caption. In the family portrait, customers see continuity with the past, reliability in the present, and sustainability for the future.

Succession is now one of the hottest topics in the corporate world. Just a few years ago, succession in organizational behavior carried the stigma of "inbreeding." Conscious efforts were made to keep new ideas coming and fresh blood flowing through the recruitment of outsiders. With the advent of international businesses involving complex organizations and highly specialized operations, however, corporations can no longer count on the recruitment of outside talent when leadership is needed or rely upon an informal system of selection within the organization by which the "cream rises to the top." Succession planning is now a well-structured process that "focuses on systematically identifying, training, evaluating and mentoring promising internal candidates."[1]

One international business, for instance, had a brilliant founder and CEO who annually hosted a retreat for potential leaders and personally made his selection based upon impression and intuition. As the company grew into global dimensions of size and specialization the informal and personalized process of handpicking leaders by the CEO no longer worked. Against resistance and skepticism a succession plan and process were put into place for identifying, recruiting, developing, and promoting persons who had the potential for top leadership roles. Today, few corporations are without such a plan and process.

In the annals of church history, the word *succession* comes with baggage. The dogma of apostolic succession, central to Roman Catholic, Eastern Orthodox, and Anglican communions, draws the line of ecclesiastical authority for bishops of the church directly from the apostles of Jesus Christ. Because the plan for apostolic succession does not always include qualifications of character and competence for the recipient, some chapters of church history are blemished by the stories of popes and bishops claiming apostolic succession while disgracing the name of Christ. These abuses may help explain why there is some reluctance to adopt the idea of "succession" as part of the thinking about Christian leadership, especially in our Protestant and evangelical traditions.

Succession Renewed

Succession is a word that deserves to be renewed in our understanding of Christian leadership. To be complete, leadership development in either a religious or secular context is a cycle of three stages—selection, service, and succession. Each of these stages is distinguished by a defining question and a specific expectation.

---

1. Bornstein, "Succession Planning," 30.

Stage I: Selection

"What do we expect a person to bring to Christian leadership?" Thousands of words have been written in books and millions of dollars spent in executive searches attempting to answer this question. The result is usually a profile of leadership that includes expectations about character, competence, and culture. Christian organizations give first priority to *character*. A Christian leader is expected to have the baseline qualities of integrity and authenticity upon which biblical faith, spiritual maturity, and consistent behavior are built. *Competence* follows, with expectations that a Christian leader meets the highest standards of educational preparation and professional certification for the announced position. Evidence is then required to show that the person has been effective in putting this knowledge and these skills into practice as an executive leader. Special attention is also given to the candidate's proof or potential for handling the complexity of the organization as well as the scope and scale of leadership. Once qualified by character and competence, *culture* enters into the equation. Is there a "fit" between the character and competence of the individual and the leadership needs of the organization? For instance, is the individual's sense of mission and vision consistent with the history, theology, and philosophy of the organization? Is the leadership style of the candidate compatible with the culture of the community? Are there background or behavioral differences that could influence leadership effectiveness? Is there a "fit" between spouse and family for the new position? Even though there is no way to assure that all of these corporate nuances are covered, it is expected that the most delicate questions will be asked. So, in answer to the opening question, *"What do we expect a person to bring to Christian leadership?,"* the answer is an exacting and probing profile of character, competence, and culture.

Stage II: Service

"What do we expect a person to do in leadership?" After going through the rigors of the search process, there is a tendency to relax expectations for performance in leadership. This is good if it means that the leader is given freedom by the board of the organization to "Go until we say stop" rather than pulling tightly the reins of "Stop until we say go." The tendency, however, is to relax the discipline of performance expectations until there is a crisis, a contract expires, or the leader asks for a review.

At one time an executive leader served "at the pleasure of the board" with only a handshake or letter of engagement. As a person who served three institutional presidencies for thirty-three years without a contract, I know how the spirit of trust between the parties is all-important. The problem is that the executive may be working against hidden expectations by which performance is judged. The annual review of an employee by his boss in a *Dilbert* cartoon exposes the dilemma.

> Employee: "I'm happy to report that I achieved every goal you set for me last year."
>
> Boss: "But you failed to achieved the secret goals I set for you."
>
> Employee: "Why would you have secret goals for me?"
>
> Boss: "For this exact situation."[2]

In such circumstances, the employee has no formal recourse for response. Consequently, elaborate contracts are now written to define the leader–board relationship, including stipulations for formal and periodic review of performance. The review process usually turns on one-year, three-year and five-year cycles. On the one-year cycle the leader announces annual goals for performance based upon a longer-term strategic plan and expects the board to review that performance in an executive session dedicated to that task. Then, every three to five years, a more formal review of leadership performance is planned involving stakeholders both within and without the organization. A consultant may be engaged to guide the process. Most often, the results of the formal review are used as a basis for renewing and rewriting the leader's contract for another three- or five-year term. As noted earlier, boards are often lax in this process or consider it pro forma unless there is a crisis involved. By and large, performance review of an incumbent leader is less exacting than the profile of expectations by which the individual was initially engaged. Character weighs heaviest among expectations in the initial profile, while competence has priority in the review of an incumbent leader's performance. Even more realistically and at the gut level, one Christian leader summed up his performance review by saying, "We are hired for our strengths and judged on our weaknesses."

---

2. *Dilbert*.

Stage III: Succession

"What do we expect a person to leave from leadership?" The expectations for the selection and service stages of the leadership cycle are very clear. In the selection of Christian leaders we ask about character with the question, *"What does this person bring to leadership?"* In the service stage we inquire about competence with the query, *"What does this person do in leadership?"* The cycle is not complete until we add the stage of succession and ask the question, *"What does this person leave from leadership?"* Because we have not adequately defined the expectations for succession in Christian leadership development, a vacuum is created. Into the empty space flow the secular standards of success. Personal status trumps institutional mission; achievements outweigh relationships; competence overrides character; past counts more than future; expediency threatens sustainability, short-term gains count more than long-term goals, and "getting" cancels out "giving." Christian leadership development is incomplete without the stage of succession, based upon an expectation as clear as "character" in selection and "competence" in service.

I propose that "continuity" be the expectation for succession in the leadership development process. Joining with character for selection and competence for service, the expectation of continuity for succession will be a pervading influence throughout the whole of leadership development.

The importance of continuity in leadership development comes home to us when we remember that succession was the primary goal of Jesus in the development of his disciples. Consistent with the three stages of the leadership cycle, Jesus saw his disciples progress through selection, service, and succession. Each stage is framed within the Father's redemptive purpose. In the selection stage Jesus chooses his disciples based upon their character for the mission; in the service stage, he works to develop their competence in mission; and in the succession stage, he counts on them for continuity of the mission after he is gone. The legacy of Christ's leadership is written not in the glitter of success, but in the gifts of succession.

2

The Prayer of Succession

"Father, the time has come. Glorify your son
that your son might glorify you."

JOHN 17:1

WHENEVER I ENCOUNTER A question that challenges the way I view my role as a Christian leader, I am driven back to the source, namely Jesus Christ himself. Searching through Scripture, I find a world of new meaning in what is called the High Priestly Prayer of Jesus in John 17. When I read the prayer through the lens of legacy for Christian leaders, I see it as the final report of Jesus to his Father before going to the cross and trusting his disciples, present and future, with the continuation and completion of his redemptive mission. In this sense, John 17 can be called the Prayer of Succession because it addresses the three questions of the Succession Principle: (1) *"What does Jesus bring to his leadership?"* (2) *"What does Jesus do in his leadership?"* and (3) *"What does Jesus leave from his leadership?"* The response comes back in three parts:

Part I—The Legacy of Trust (vv. 1–5)

Part II—The Legacy of Truth (vv. 6–19)

Part III—The Legacy of Love (vv. 20–26)

By searching for the answers to the leadership questions through the legacy that Jesus left in his final prayer, we may well discover the correctives that we need to change our thinking from the secular meaning of success to the spiritual meaning of succession.

The Legacy of Trust

What does Jesus bring to his leadership? In Part I of his prayer (John 17:1–5) Jesus reports directly to his Father. He does not make any claim to name, title, status, or position. Rather, with an eye always fixed on the Father's mission, Jesus accounts for the "authority over all people" entrusted to him by the Father. He reports that he has exercised his authority exclusively to address the contamination of human sin and "give eternal life to all those you have given him" (v. 2). At this point, we would expect him to report his successes. Instead, he bows before the Father as the "only true God," (v. 3) acknowledging that he has no authority of his own, but serves only at the will of the Father ("The Gift of Authority," chapter 3).

Continuing, Jesus reports that he has glorified the Father by "completing the work you gave me to do" (v. 4). No credit is taken for specific achievements, but behind the statement is the competence with which Jesus organized, coordinated, and implemented every detail to complete his earthly task. In management terms, Jesus' purpose, policies, and practices are all aligned with the strategic challenge of human redemption and focused on his holy task ("The Gift of Accomplishment," chapter 4).

With clarity of authority and coherence of administration, Jesus can now claim closure for the legacy of trust that the Father bestowed upon his Son. Summing up his personal report, Jesus accounts for his stewardship of all the resources—physical and spiritual, personal and interpersonal—entrusted to him, by saying, "I have brought you glory on earth" (v. 4). Nothing more needs to be done. Jesus rests his case and puts himself back into the hands of God: "Father, glorify me in your presence with the glory I had with you before the world began" ("The Gift of Accountability," chapter 5).

Viewing these facts from a leadership perspective, we see that God the Father's grand strategy for human redemption is the basis for assessing the legacy of Jesus' ministry. Everything turns on his exercise of the authority given to him by the Father to bring eternal life to all humanity, his competence in administering the details to bring that task to completion, and his confidence in reporting to the Father that he has glorified him on earth by fulfilling his mission. Notably, Jesus says that he has completed the specific task assigned to him. Even though there is no eternal life without his self-sacrifice, there are other tasks to be completed and other players in the redemptive drama. The story will go on in the leadership of his disciples, present and future, who are also being invested with authority to complete the task given to them and to glorify God. Without him, without them, and without us, the plan for eternal life is not complete.

The legacy of trust that Jesus leaves us comes home in questions that we must answer as Christian leaders:

1. How have we exercised the leadership authority that God has entrusted to us for his purpose of bringing eternal life to all people?

2. How have we organized and implemented the required functions in order to coordinate and complete our task?

3. How have we accounted for the physical, human, and spiritual resources entrusted to us in order to give the glory to God?

Our answers to these questions will determine our legacies as leaders in the name of Christ. Our legacies will be written not in terms of our name, title, position, or status, but by exercising our authority, completing our task, and accepting our accountability for glorifying God.

The Legacy of Truth

What does Jesus do in his leadership? The question immediately triggers thoughts about tangible achievements that can be measured by impressive statistics and visible success. As usual, we are wrong. Jesus brings the Father's word of truth to his leadership in order to develop mature disciples, not to achieve secular success. The legacy of truth will be written in the readiness of his disciples to assume leadership in his place (John 17:6–19).

As the Father invests Jesus with authority for his mission, he also entrusts him with the word of truth for his relationship with his disciples. Faithful to his trust, Jesus reports to the Father that he "gave them words you gave me and they accepted them" (John 17:8). With these words, Jesus is laying claim to the highest level of outcomes for the teaching-learning process ("The Gift of Assimilation," chapter 6). He is saying that his disciples have internalized the word of truth, made it their own, and are ready to communicate it to others. Multiple results follow when Jesus' teaching of the word of truth is internalized in his hearers. One result is the *certainty* with which the disciples believe that Jesus came from the Father and was sent by the Father (John 17:8). Another result is Jesus' *confidence* that the disciples are now identified as one with him and the Father (John 17:9). The final confirmation, then, is in the glory that comes to Jesus through the seal of their faith and the oneness of their relationship (John 17:10). Assured that his disciples are grounded in the word of truth and matured in their spiritual understanding, Jesus is like a mother bird ready to push her brood out of the nest ("The Gift of Assurance," chapter 7).

Jesus' legacy of truth then shifts from the spiritual maturity of the disciples to the reality that they will remain in the world as his successors. In preparation for the transition, Jesus is willing to risk the power of the name given to him by the Father as the name by which the disciples will be known (John 17:11–12). By the name of Jesus they have been protected and kept safe, except for Judas, the "one doomed to destruction so that the Scripture would be fulfilled" (John 17:12). Now, because they bear his name, they will be hated by the world just as Jesus was hated. But hate cannot triumph. In honor of their faithfulness, there is reserved for them the "full measure of joy" (John 17:13) that only their Master knew ("The Gift of Affirmation," chapter 8).

From his own experience Jesus also knows his disciples will be under constant attack by the "evil one" (John 17:15). As we have already seen, their ultimate protection against the archenemy will be the word of truth and the name of Christ. But, just as in Jesus' case, external protection must be complemented by internal purity. To assure that end, Jesus prays, "Sanctify them through thy truth: thy word is truth" (John 17:17). This is not enough. In keeping with his lifelong submission to the discipline of God's word, Jesus once more opens himself to its purifying power with his disciples in mind: "I sanctify myself that they too may be truly sanctified" (John 17:19). By personalizing his prayer and modeling his message, Jesus gives us the highest and best definition of Christian leadership ("The Gift of Anointing," chapter 9).

The legacy of truth applies to all Christian leaders. When the time comes for us to step aside in favor of our successor, these questions will remain:

1. Have our followers internalized the word of truth entrusted to us for teaching in principle and practice?

2. Have our followers the assurance of faith that comes with their identity in the name of the Father and the Son?

3. Have our followers experienced the full measure of Christ's joy whatever the circumstances?

4. Have our followers seen our example and submitted themselves to the sanctifying discipline of the word of truth?

Humbling questions, to be sure. All of our professional achievements as leaders take a distant second place to the personal and spiritual development of our disciples whom God has entrusted to us. The penultimate test of our leadership is found in the question, "How do our followers handle the word of truth?"

The Legacy of Love

What does Jesus leave from his leadership? Usually, when we answer this question, we look back on the past and focus on the success of the individual. Jesus does just the opposite. He sees his legacy in a forward look, with its focus upon the sustainability of his leadership through established institutions under the umbrella of his body, the church.

As background for this final section of the Prayer of Succession (John 17:20–26), Jesus assumes that he has ascended to heaven and the apostles have died by natural death or martyrdom. Who will be their successors? Jesus anticipates a body of believers who are his followers through the ministry of his disciples. In each generation to follow, then, the evidence of succession in leadership will be a company of believers who are empowered by his authority, disciplined by his word, protected by his name, and characterized by his joy ("The Gift of Anticipation," chapter 10). For them, Jesus has one final request of his Father: "May they be brought to complete unity to let the world know that you sent me and have loved them even as you have loved me" (John 17:23). No specific organizational plans are drawn but the ultimate outcome of succession in Christian leadership is certain and clear. Love is the invisible bond that holds the body of Christ together and unity is the quality that sets it apart. It is the continuing witness of his church, unified by the invisible bond of love, that is the legacy for which Jesus yearns ("The Gift of Accord," chapter 11).

Our record for sharing this legacy with Jesus is spotty. On one extreme we have stressed unity at the expense of truth; at the other extreme we have claimed a corner on truth at the expense of unity. Our problem is a soft, soggy, and shallow kind of love. This is not the love of which Jesus speaks. Deliberately using the word *agape*, Jesus defines the kind of love that the Father shows for his Son and the kind of love the Son shows for us. *Agape* love goes deeper than family, friendship, or romance—deeper than wishes of dreamers or the play-acting of pretenders. Following the example of Jesus Christ, sacrificial love means surrender without stipulation, service without success, and even suffering without support. No other love can make us one with the Father and his Son; no other love can cause a hostile world to sit up and take notice ("The Gift of *Agape*," chapter 12).

Jesus' prayer now passes to us. When the legacy of our leadership is written, what will we leave to our successor and coming generations?

1. Do we see beyond our time and tenure to envision the full potential of the organization we are called to lead?

2. Do we leave an organization unified by the Spirit of Christ's love in complexity, diversity, and even conflict?

3. Do we bequeath to our successor the example of sacrificial love in surrender without stipulation, service without success, and suffering without support?

These questions force us to change our thinking from a legacy of success to a legacy of succession.

Rethinking Succession

If we take Jesus' Prayer of Succession seriously, we will have to be ready for major changes in the way we think about our legacy to those who will succeed us. We will have to:

- reverse the *direction* of our thinking about legacy. Instead of focusing on the past and our success as a leader, we should anticipate the future and our responsibility for the line of succession.

- remember that succession is a *process* in leadership development as well as a plan at the time of anticipating leadership change. The process of succession begins with the quality of trust invested in the selection of the leader, continues in the transfer of truth accomplished through the service of a leader, and comes to fulfillment in the unifying spirit of love projected forward at the time of succession.

- rethink the order of *importance* placed on our legacy according to the Succession Principle: What we bring to leadership is *important*; what we do in leadership is *more important*; what we leave from leadership is *most important of all.*

- reorder the *priorities* for the legacy we leave with succession in mind: mission takes priority over position; relationships take priority over achievements; and long-term goals take priority over short-term gains.

Dare we rethink our legacy in these terms? If we do, whether we are emerging leaders, maturing leaders, or retiring leaders, we will take our cue from the final report of Jesus to his Father and turn our attention from the glitter of success to the gifts of succession.

PART I

The Legacy of Trust

3

The Gift of Authority

"For you granted him authority over all
people that he might give eternal life to all
those you have given him."

JOHN 17:1–2

AUTHORITY IS A SACRED trust of Christian leadership. In the opening words
of the Prayer of Succession Jesus accepts that trust and the responsibility
that goes with it. Even though he is given authority over all people he uses
it only for the purpose of giving us eternal life and glorifying his Father. In
him we see how authority to lead is to be accepted humbly, used discreetly,
delegated clearly, and double-checked regularly. He leaves us this example
as the first gift of succession by answering these questions:

"What is the source of our authority?"

"What is the character of our authority?"

"What is the test of our authority?"

"How do we handle the crisis of authority?"

"What is the authority we leave to our successor?"

If we are true to our trust, we too will leave the gift of authority to those
who follow us.

The Source of His Authority

To understand the authority of Jesus we must begin with his relationship with his Father. In the opening words of his prayer he reveals the uniqueness of the Father-Son relationship. "Father, the time has come. Glorify your son that he may glorify you"(John 17:1). The mutuality of trust and love, blended into common purpose, sets the stage for everything else we learn about the authority of Jesus. There is no substitute for the person who gives authority and the person who receives it being totally invested in a common cause. Trust is the lifeline. The Father matches the authority he gives with the task he assigns to his Son. In turn, the Son honors that trust by being obedient to the Father's authority and accountable to him for the results. With the bond of this relationship they will glorify each other in fulfilling their redemptive purpose.

At the beginning of his ministry Jesus has to choose the source of his authority. In the wilderness Satan tempts him to rely upon the standard sources of human authority (Matt 4:1–11). With the temptation to turn the stones into bread, Satan coaxes Jesus to rely upon the *authority of performance*. When he dares him to leap from the pinnacle of the temple and prove that he is the Son of God, Satan offers him the *authority of position*. When the promise of the wealth and power of the kingdoms of the world is put before Jesus if he would fall down and worship Satan, he has to choose whether or not to rely upon the *authority of power*.

Why does Jesus resist these choices? He knows that each of these sources of authority has a dark and devastating downside. The *authority of performance*, for instance, has the downside of being sustained only by the escalation of achievement. As in Vince Lombardi's philosophy of football coaching—"Winning isn't everything, it is the only thing"—the moment you stop winning, you lose your authority. The *authority of position* is equally hazardous. Position authority is fragile not just because it depends upon titles, rank, and symbols of office, but also because it depends upon the acceptance of the people over whom power is held. The Queen of England, for instance, holds her authority by position. But when scandal rocked the monarchy, her authority was eroded and the people insisted that she pay taxes. The monarchy will never be the same. Respect for the authority of position has broken down in Western culture. Clergy who rely on the symbols of the title "Reverend," the clerical collar, the preaching robe, and the cross around the neck have suffered the most. A Gallup poll at the end of 2013 carries the shocking news that only 49 percent of Americans now put high trust in the clergy for "honesty and ethics" and rank them lower than nurses, pharmacists, grade school teachers, medical doctors, and military officers. In comparison, only 8 percent of the general public ranks members of Congress highly for "honesty and ethics," putting them just below used car salesmen, with lobbyists at the very bottom of the list.[1] If Jesus had relied upon his position as "the Son of God" alone, he would have suffered the loss of authority from those who rejected his title.

The *authority of power*, based upon the wealth of the kingdoms of the world, is also fleeting. In *Fortune* magazine, you can see the rise and fall of authority based upon wealth. One year at the top of the list is Bill Gates, another year it is Warren Buffett, and in another year an Arab prince beats them both. Andy Warhol had it right when he said that in the media age, "everyone will have fifteen minutes of fame." I experienced that fleeting fame when I was a leading nominee for the secretary of education in the Reagan cabinet. One moment I stood before a flood of television lights in a press conference and answered calls for interviews from the *New York Times* and the *Washington Post*. Within a few hours, however, the political winds shifted and I was left with only the memories of fleeing fame to tell my grandchildren.

Jesus makes a choice. In preparation for his ministry he rejects the authority of performance, position, and power. Like Jesus, we are also tempted to choose one or another of these sources of authority. I, for instance, don't think that the authority of position has been a problem for me. As far as I know, I have carried the titles of "Reverend" and "Doctor" rather lightly. I have never had to sign my letters, "David L. McKenna, PhD," and I don't believe I have been victimized by the problem of "Ph.Deity."

Power based upon public acclaim has also been handled fairly well. In a teaching experience at the Cove in Asheville, North Carolina, I found myself the center of attention for 200 people who seemed to project the aura of Billy Graham onto me. I had to stop eating in the dining room and walking through the lobby because of the way the people seemed to fawn after me. When one woman came up and said, "Let me just touch you," I fled.

The authority of performance is my temptation. Coming from a blue-collar home in the Depression era with parents who had not graduated from high school, the drive to achieve advanced degrees and realize visionary goals is both my strength and my weakness. Robert Wuthnow, the Princeton sociologist who is an astute observer of the contemporary American

---

1. *Gallup Politics*, "Honesty and Ethics Rating of Clergy Slides to New Low."

religious scene, writes that the authority of the clergy is now judged by achievement and warns us about the downside of a competitive spirit, a market mentality, and ego–driven motives.[2] I must heed his warning.

Jesus had a choice of authority just as we do. When the people of Capernaum said, "He taught as one having authority, and not as the scribes" (Matt 7:29), they were astonished because his authority did not come from the standard sources of ascription, achievement, or acclaim. What then was the authority that Jesus claimed for his ministry?

The Character of His Authority

A man who has come to worship in the synagogue is possessed by an un-clean spirit. As Jesus begins to speak, the demon cries out, "Let us alone! What have we to do with you Jesus of Nazareth? Did you come to destroy us? I know who you are—the Holy One of God!" (Mark 1:24).

We have the answer to our question. Jesus backs up the authority over all people given him by his Father with the *authority of character*. Even the demons saw in his holiness the mirror image of the holy God. C. S. Lewis describes a Christian as a person who has "a fragrance that is not our own but borrowed, in becoming clean mirrors filled with the image of a face that is not ours."[3] His thought echoes the passage in 2 Corinthians 3:18, where Paul wrote, "And we, who with unveiled faces all reflecting the Lord's glory, are being transformed into his likeness with ever-increasing glory, which comes from the Lord, who is the Spirit . . ." The transformation is not im-mediate, but the authority gained by being transformed into his likeness is the only authority that is not dependent upon position, performance, or power. The demons knew it and so must we.

To choose a holy character as our authority for leadership comes with a price. In one of his novels Dostoyevsky tells the story of Prince Myshkin, a Christ figure. Prince Myshkin is born into a culture obsessed with wealth, power, and sex. But he has no greed for money, no drive for power, and no lust for sex. His innocence and simplicity lead people to believe that he is abnormal. But Dostoyevsky portrays Prince Myshkin as a truly beautiful soul. But how does the world perceive him? The answer is in the title of Dostoyevsky's novel. It is called *The Idiot*. Wholeness of heart, simplicity of soul, and singleness of mind—the qualities of holiness—are still abnormal

2. Wuthnow, *Christianity in the 21st Century*, 51.

3. Lewis, "Becoming Clean Mirrors," 39.

sources of authority in a society driven by the motives of ascribed titles, achieved expertise, and acclaimed public confidence.

The Use of His Authority

Leaders reveal who they are by the way they use their authority. A major reason for a younger generation losing its trust in established leadership is abuse or corruption in the exercise of authority. Overuse is seen in leaders who flaunt their authority to dominate and manipulate; abuse is rampant in the exercise of authority for personal or political advantage; and erosion is evident when authority gives way to social pressure and political correctness. When Jesus reports to the Father on how he exercised the authority entrusted to him, he gives us a set of principles to assure the integrity of our leadership and to leave intact the gift of authority to our successors.

Jesus humbly accepts the authority that the Father entrusts to him. With "authority over all people" Jesus had absolute power for controlling, commanding, and judging human behavior. At any given moment he could have exercised that authority. In the temptation, angels could have put a safety net under him as he plunged from the pinnacle of the temple. With righteous anger after witnessing firsthand the sins of a Sodomic society, he could have rained down fire and brimstone. At the cross he could have commanded legions of angels to rescue him. In none of these instances did he invoke the ultimate authority of control, command, and judgment that had been given to him. For us, this is a rare show of humility. With pride, we not only exercise all the authority given to us, but also, with arrogance, we even presume authority that we do not have. Jesus shows us the better way. The authority that we receive for Christian leadership must be accepted with humility and exercised with discretion.

Jesus uses his authority to fulfill the Father's redemptive purpose. Authority is always given for a specific task within a larger purpose. The president of an organization, for instance, is granted executive authority within the policy of the board in order to fulfill the purpose for which the organization exists. This plan becomes the basis for judging the effectiveness of the organization through its board and chief executive officer. In the case of Jesus, the grand plan for human redemption is the purpose of the Godhead: the Father is the policy maker and the holder of authority; Jesus is the Son authorized as the one sacrificing himself for the sins of all people; and the Holy Spirit is the agent continuing the truth, righteousness, and judgment of Christ through to completion. In the Prayer of Succession, Jesus accepts the Father's plan, authority, and assignment like a son of whom a father is most proud. He does not dwell on the cost to himself but looks forward to "eternal life" for all those given to him as they will know the Father as "the only true God," and himself whom the Father has sent (John 17:3). Authority takes on a different cast in this picture. Control, command, and judgment give way to obedience, sacrifice, and joy. The challenge is before us.

Jesus used his authority with discretion and never for personal, political, or economic advantage. We have noted that Jesus could have summoned legions of angels to rescue him on the cross or called fire and brimstone down upon a sinful city. He also used his authority to predict future judgment upon Jerusalem for rejecting him and did not hesitate to speak woes upon corrupt scribes and Pharisees who deceived the people. Few of us would have had his restraint when he was personally accused of drunkenness (Matt 11:19), blasphemy (Matt 26:65), insanity (Mark 3:21), demon-possession (John 7:20), Sabbath breaking (John 9:16), and treason (John 19:12). We feel most deeply for him, however, when he is rejected by his family and the citizens of Nazareth, his hometown (Luke 4:28–29). We feel the anguish and share the pain that Jesus must have felt when his family and friends in the synagogue at Nazareth "drove him out of town, and took him to the brow of the hill on which the town was built, in order to throw him down the cliff" (Luke 4:28). The fact that "he walked right through the crowd and went on his way" (Luke 4:30) doesn't help much. He leaves town with a broken heart.

Jesus also encounters the politics of Rome in tests of authority. When the Pharisees try to suck him into the trap of pledging allegiance either to Herod or to God, he uses his wit rather than his wrath. "Give to Caesar what belongs to Caesar and to God what belongs to God" (Matt 22:21) has gone down in history as the declaration that dumbfounded his critics. Still later, when standing before Pilate, he is asked, "Are you the King of the Jews?" (Matt 27:11). To answer "Yes" would have been self-incriminating. Instead, Jesus turns the question back to Pilate in a way that implies "Yes" but cannot be incriminating. "You said it" leaves Pilate with no evidence of insurrection. True to his trust, Jesus lives and serves without using his ultimate authority to carry his own case.

Jesus delegates authority to his disciples with clarity and confidence. Every leader knows that authority is a delicate and dangerous resource. It is delicate because its exercise requires an artist's touch, paying attention to texture, tone, and color in its application. It is dangerous because it can be overused to the detriment of organizational purpose or eroded by weakness under pressure. Jesus teaches us how to delegate authority when he chooses his twelve disciples and shares with them the authority "to drive out evil spirits and to heal every disease and sickness" (Matt 10:1). With the delegation goes the trust that lets his followers learn and grow on their own.

Every leader needs checks on authority. Whether by attention or inattention, the authority that we are given for leadership can be overused, underused, or misdirected. What is the check and balance we need? Good practices for organizational behavior set up safeguards for a balance of power between policy-making boards and decision-making executives. Governmental agencies draw strict lines of balanced authority among judicial, legislative, and executive branches. These same safeguards need to be brought into the constitutional framework for any organization. Because of the weight of emphasis upon character in Christian organizations, the balance of power tips easily to personalities. The imbalance can be fatal to the organization and a disgrace to the kingdom of God. From personal experience as a youngster growing up in an independent, holiness tabernacle under the domination of a charismatic leader, I know the power of personality. The fire of hell loomed over any deviation from his authority, especially for a vulnerable teenager. Later, as a college president, I learned how an unchecked higher authority can break the trust of executive leadership. I also know the moment when I overstepped the lines of authority and deserved the discipline of the board.

Authority is the most delicate of relationships. How can we keep it in check? Jesus gives us the answer in his prior commitment to the glory of God. Time and time again, Christian leaders must stop, assess their achievements, and ask, "Who is glorified, God or me?" The answer will be self-evident. If we are leading in the will of God, the results will be to the glory of God. Dare we ask our followers, "As you see how I use my authority, who is glorified, God or me?" Most of us do not want to ask that question. We might get an honest answer.

The Crisis of Authority

Christian leadership depends on the authority of character. A holy character is the only authority that will win in the contest with evil. After the demon cries out, "I know who you are, the Holy One of God!" Jesus rebukes him, "Be quiet and come out of him." With the expulsion of evil, the people are even more amazed and buzz among themselves, "What is this? A new teaching—and with authority! He even gives orders to evil spirits and they obey Him." (Mark 1:27). In the contest with evil, authority based on performance, position, or power will fail. At best, we can only win a Pyrrhic victory. It was Pyrrhus, Greek King of Epirus, who looked over a battlefield at the number of his fallen troops and declared, "If we are victorious in one more battle with the Romans, we shall be utterly ruined."[4] The contest between Christ and culture must never become a Pyrrhic battlefield. If we rely on the authority of the human weapons of performance, position, or power, we may win some battles but lose the war.

Among Isaiah's magnificent metaphors, one stands out in the sixty-third chapter of his prophecy. A watchman on the wall looks out to see a victorious warrior approaching the gates. He calls out, "Who is this, robed in splendor, striding forward in the greatness of his strength?" The answer comes back, "It is I, speaking in righteousness, ready to save." Again the watchman calls out, "Why are your garments red, like those of one treading the winepress?" The bloodstained victor responds, "I have trodden the winepress alone, from the nations no one was with me" (Isaiah 63:1–3). This is the image of Jesus Christ in his mortal battle with the forces of evil. He is victorious, but not without bloodstained garments, and not without the righteousness of character by which he stands alone with no one to help him.

I need not remind you that we too are locked in mortal conflict with the forces of evil. It is moral warfare when 160,000 children stay home from school each day for fear of being shot. It is ethical warfare when science can clone human beings through genetic engineering. It is spiritual warfare when the sports–entertainment complex replaces the military–industrial–educational complex as the creator of values and the antagonist of faith. Just as real as Paul's "principalities and powers," we are in a life-and-death struggle with evil today. If we rely upon the weapons of the world—performance, position, or power—we will lose, because Satan can always out-perform us, out-position us, and out-power us.

With biting humor in Acts 13:19, we read the story of the seven sons of Sceva, apostate Jews who make mockery of Jesus' name by trying to drive out demons. They say, "In the name of Jesus whom Paul preaches, I command you to come out." The evil spirit however, answers, "Jesus I know, and

4. "Pyrrhus," *Wikipedia.*

Paul I know, but who are you?" Then the man possessed by the evil spirit jumps on them and gives them such a beating that they run from the house naked and bleeding. Without the authority of holy character in the contest with evil, we become the punchlines of demons' jokes.

In Barbara Tuchman's book *The March of Folly*, she verifies the historical disaster that followed the reign of six popes who corrupted their authority in the fifteenth century, preceding the Protestant Reformation. At the same time that the Renaissance in art, music, and architecture was bringing beauty to an ugly world, the Renaissance popes wallowed in the sins of indulgence and immorality. According to Tuchman, the corruption of their character led them to the folly of "wooden-headedness" in refusing to heed the urgent plea of the laity for reform in the church.[5] Finally, there was no alternative other than Martin Luther laying down the gauntlet at the Diet of Worms with the declaration of protest and separation, "Here I stand, so help me God." Tuchman's point is that the abuse of authority by the corruption of character split the church and changed the world. The warning of history echoes through all of the years that follow. Power without virtue is the path to disaster. Power with virtue, however, is the promise of greater things given to us by Jesus Christ.

The Gift of Authority

What are the gifts of authority that you will leave to your successor? The Prayer of Succession gives us our guide. A Christian leader who follows the example of Jesus will leave his or her successor:

1. An *obedient authority* in relationship with a higher authority working together toward a common purpose;

2. A *humble authority* exercised with discretion for an assigned task and never for personal or political advantage;

3. A *tested authority* with integrity in moral crisis;

4. A *delegated authority* to followers based upon clear lines and specific functions;

5. A *monitored authority* assuring its use for the glory of God.

Undergirding these gifts is the authority of character. Without the gift of a holy life, all other gifts lose their meaning.

5. Tuchman, *The March of Folly*, 7–8.

The truth of this message gets updated almost daily in news reports. In 1993, for instance, *Time* magazine featured Billy Graham on the cover along with the lead article, "A Christian in Winter—Billy Graham at 75." Even after forty-six years of scrutiny under the white-hot lamp of public recognition and media investigation, the article summed up Billy's career with this conclusion: "Evangelical Protestantism has triumphed over other sugar-coated brands, not least because [Billy Graham's] sincerity and probity protected his movement from the stain spread by the moral and financial disasters of other high-wattage clerics."[6] Under criticism or in crisis, there is no substitute for the authority of character.

Our own personal Pentecost is a purifying as well as an empowering experience. We have emphasized its inner cleansing and its outer witness. The Scripture texts for this chapter remind us that a personal Pentecost is also the source of authority for our leadership. Holiness is the only spiritual weapon with which we can be victors in the mortal battle that we will face with the principalities and powers of the forces of evil. Two questions remain with us: *"What authority will we claim for our leadership?"* and *"What authority will we leave from our leadership?"* Of all the gifts of succession that follow, none is more delicate than the authority we claim and the authority we leave. If the authority of God's holy trust is complemented by the authority of holy character, great good will follow. If, however, the authority of trust is violated or the authority of character is contaminated, great evil can follow. Before considering any other gift of succession, a Christian leader must stop and ask, "Am I leaving my successor the gift of the authority of trust conferred by God and the authority of character confirmed by his Spirit?"

6. "A Christian in Winter—Billy Graham at 75."

4

The Gift of Accomplishment

"I have glorified you on earth by completing
the work that you gave me to do."

JOHN 17:4

ACROSS THE WIDE SPECTRUM of the Christian community, we have heard an urgent call for the development of leaders. Have you ever heard anyone make a similar plea for the development of managers? Everyone wants to be a leader, but few would confess that they want to be a manager. In our scramble to develop Christian leaders, the gift of administration is relegated to second place.

A delightful story is told about two men who died and whose funerals were scheduled on the same day and at the same time. The undertaker made the mistake of mixing up the favorite suits of the men in which they were to be buried. When one of the widows arrived just before the funeral service she took one look in the coffin and went into hysteria. "That's not my husband's suit. What happened to it?" Instantly, the undertaker realized his mistake and the fact that it was too late to change the suits on the two bodies. What would he do? After a moment's hesitation the mechanics of his mortician's mind came up with the answer. Putting his arm around the sobbing widow, he calmly said, "Don't worry, my dear, we will just change heads."

This apocryphal story exposes one of the flaws in succession plans drawn up by boards in times of transition. It is often assumed that a change of heads will cover any mistakes and solve all problems. Put another way, it is assumed that good management inevitably follows great leadership.

Peter Drucker may have inadvertently contributed to this viewpoint in the words attributed to him and co-opted by Bennis and Nanus in their book, *Leaders*: "Managers are people who do things right and leaders are people who do the right things."[1] Tacitly, at least, Drucker seems to imply that leadership trumps management on the scale of value and position. But knowing Drucker's reputation as the "Father of Modern Management," we can be sure that he means a complementary and integrative relationship between two different dimensions of administration. Even more important, as Bob Buford quickly discovered in his conversations with Drucker, "His real business—his primary interest in management—is not for the sake of business itself, but the for the people it touches, serves and influences."[2]

Don't blame Drucker. The idea that leadership trumps management has its roots in another source. As leadership has been popularized it has taken on the glamor of lofty vision, charismatic character, and entrepreneurial drama. Management, then, comes off with the image of a corporate Walter Mitty, hunkering down in a computerized cubicle, wearing a green eyeshade, and counting beans. No wonder young people say, "I want to be a leader and do the right things." Have you ever heard one counter, "I want to be a manager and do things right"? Yet, as I know from experience, managers are unsung servants who make a leader look good and, often, far better than he or she is.

One of the managers I esteem is James Brumfield, controller at Asbury Theological Seminary during my administration, who continues to serve my successors. Jim doesn't give speeches and he is not front-and-center in public events, but when it comes to controlling a budget of many millions and reporting on an endowment of multimillions more, you know that he is as sure and steady as the rising sun. Whenever I asked Jim a question about finance, he either had the answer or found it right away. Jim's faithful service at Asbury Seminary tells us why Jesus defined a steward within the definition of the word "economics" or *oikonomos*, meaning a person who is entrusted to preserve and enact the laws or norms of the household. No one

1. Bennis and Nanus, *Leaders*, 21.
2. Buford, *Drucker and Me*, 42.

can ever doubt that Jim's stewardship of "doing things right" is a ministry indispensable to effective leadership.

Downgrading management is not biblical. A leader cannot do the right things without a manager who does things right. Every organization is first judged by the standards of best practices as the baseline for managerial integrity and efficiency. History is replete with the sad stories of visionary and charismatic leaders whose careers were derailed by cooked books, nefarious scams, and self-aggrandizing expenditures. Great leaders are dependent upon good managers. The relationship cannot be denied. So, when Jesus reports on the "work" that the Father gave him to do, we get the sense that he knew the grit of management as well as the glory of leadership. From an organizational standpoint he may also be anticipating the revelation given to Paul of the organic body of Christ, in which all the diverse parts are interdependent and functioning together. From this perspective, then, administration in an organization takes its place among the essential gifts given by God if the body of Christ is to function efficiently and witness effectively in the world. One of the best compliments I received as an administrator came from a seminary trustee who described our board meetings as "smooth as riding in a Mercedes with the engine purring." Behind the compliment were hours, days, and weeks of work coordinating all of the components of administrative action in support of the strategic plan and its goals. Even in administration there is a sense of artistry that comes together when planning, organizing, staffing, coordinating, reporting, and budgeting are in sync with purpose, goals, and strategy. Another look at the biblical model for organization, in which leadership and management become one in the succession process, is well worth our time.

The Coherent Body of Christ

For the book *A Celebration of Ministry*, a festschrift honoring the presidency of Frank Bateman Stanger at Asbury Theological Seminary, I was asked to write a chapter on "Administration as Ministry."[3] To do this, I took 1 Corinthians 12 apart and put it back together again in eight working principles of administration:

1. God, through the Holy Spirit, is the founder of the church, the center of its organization, and the source of all spiritual gifts (1 Cor 12:3–6).

---

3. Kinghorn, ed., *A Celebration of Ministry*, 70–79.

2. Members of the church, by the same Holy Spirit, have different gifts, ministries, and operating styles (1 Cor 12:4–6).

3. God, through the Holy Spirit, endows each person with one of his special gifts: wisdom, knowledge, faith, healing, miracles, prophecy, discernment, tongues, or interpretation of tongues (1 Cor 12:7–11).

4. God, through the Holy Spirit, gives different gifts, ministries, and operating styles to different people for the common good (1 Cor 12:7).

5. All of the diverse gifts, ministries, and styles in the body of Christ are integral to its harmony and essential to its effectiveness (1 Cor 12:12–27).

6. God, through the Holy Spirit, organizes the church by appointing to special office apostles, prophets, and teachers, and to special work healers, helpers, administrators, and speakers in tongues (1 Cor. 12:27–28).

7. Whatever general or special gift the Holy Spirit gives a person, higher gifts can be sought and received (1 Cor 12:28–31).

8. Love is the highest gift of the Holy Spirit, available to all, and indispensable to the internal harmony and external effectiveness of the body of Christ (1 Cor 12:31).

These principles confirm the fact that the core of the term *organization* is "organic." Even though the combined term "organic organization" is redundant, it is needed as a reminder that the model for the communal body of Christ is unified in diversity and coherent in function.

The Unity of Function

Is administration a ministry? Theoretically, an affirmative answer may seem obvious, but practically, we cancel the answer when we tip the scale of Christian vocation from the horizontal to the vertical plane and read a "pecking order" into Paul's description of special offices, such as apostles, prophets, and teachers; and special work, including healers, helpers, administrators, and speakers in tongues. True, the division of labor includes primary functions that we identify with leaders and support functions that we identify with management. But these differences must be put into the context of: (1) the oneness of a special gift for every person; (2) the goal of the common good; (3) the harmony essential to effectiveness; (4) the potential for every person to gain greater gifts; and (5) love, the greatest gift of all. A vertical pecking order based upon title, specialization, or pride has no place in the organic body of Christ.

Long ago, a pipe organ needed someone to pump the bellows behind the scenes so that the instrument could be played. One concert artist was notoriously known for his exaggerated ego. When he took his bows and responded to standing ovations from his audience, he filled the air with "I" upon "I" of self-exaltation. After one concert in which he was particularly obnoxious, he sat back down at the organ to play an encore. Adjusting his seat, flipping his tails, primping his hair, and dancing his hands high in the air, he came down with a flourish on the keyboard. Nothing happened. With a look of surprise, he went through the motions again and struck the keys. Again, nothing happened. Surprise turned to anger as he tried for the third time. Racing around behind the organ, he found the boy whose job was to pump the bellows. With white-hot rage he screamed, "Who do you think you are? You have just ruined the finest concert of the greatest organist in the world." With cold calm the boy of the bellows answered, "Say 'we,' mister."

Likewise, in the body of Christ, the word is "we." However the church may be organized by position, role, and function, there is no room for the exalted "I." *E Pluribus Unum* raised to nth power by the Holy Spirit should be on the seal of every Christian organization. In this context, the special gift and work of administration takes on new meaning. Management is more than efficiency of functions; it is all about the effectiveness of relationships. With the story of the election of the seven deacons as our model in Acts 6:1–7, nine premises give us insight into the "work" that Jesus was given to do.

Stewardship Is Our Calling

First, *stewardship* is the special calling of administration. Waiting on tables is not a glamorous job, but when the apostles called the community together and said, "Brothers, choose seven men among you," they set them apart, called them to a holy task, and gave them responsibility for administration (Acts 6:3–4). The derivative meaning of the word *administration* is "to steer," with the visual image of a helmsman guiding a ship through the seas or into a harbor. On our daily walk we often see a neighbor named Jim whose bearded visage and nautical cap identifies him as a harbor master for the port of Anchorage, Alaska. As the liners, cruisers, and oilers approach the port, Jim takes over the helm and pilots the ships to dock through waters that can be treacherous for a captain who does not know the quirks of the tides, currents, narrows, and hazards of the harbor. While the captain may be the one who is credited for bringing the ship to its destination by doing the right things, it is Jim, an anonymous helmsman, who assures the completion of a safe voyage by doing things right. The cruise ship that went aground off the coast of Sicily is a tragic reminder that a captain who does not pay attention to the whimsy of a tricky tide is a danger to his ship, his passengers, and his cargo. "Aha," we might say, "the devil is in the details," but the fact is that this familiar idiom is a twist on the viewpoint of our ancestors, who said, "God is in the details." At its highest and best, administration is a calling to show how God is at work in the details. Eugene Peterson's interpretation of John 17:4 in *The Message* carries the same thought when he has Jesus saying to the Father, "I glorified you on earth By completing down to the last detail What you assigned me to do."

Power Is Our Resource

Second, *power* is the special resource of administration. After the election of the seven deacons for waiting on tables and resolving the widows' complaints, the apostles said to the company, "We will turn this responsibility over to them and will give our attention to prayer and the ministry of the word" (Acts 6:3–4). This decision is administration at its best. Power, with full confidence along with full responsibility, is turned over to the deacons as an example of administration delegation.

In its simplest and perhaps purest definition, power means "the ability to influence others."[4] Within that broad definition, however, the idea of power ranges all the way from the gift of God exercised for his glory and the common good to the tool of Machiavelli wielded for dictatorial dominance and absolute corruption. Because the abuses of power are in the daily news and everyone has a personal story confirming abuse, our natural leaning is to equate power with the negatives of control and manipulation. Anyone who has been a victim of a bureaucrat who uses a smidgen of power to make us feel small knows what I mean. Even after Adolf Hitler achieved dictatorial power in Nazi Germany, he could not control a government accountant who would not pay him his pension from serving as a corporal

---

4. *The American Heritage Dictionary.*

in the army during World War I. Hitler went to his grave without getting his money. After I had an encounter with an IRS agent who would not answer my questions until he had reduced me to a cipher, even Hitler has my sympathy.

Andy Crouch counters our negative experiences with power brokers in his book *Playing God: Redeeming the Gift of Power*. Rather than assuming that power is a neutral or negative force, he takes the Genesis view that power is one of God's special gifts to humankind intended for partnering in the creative process.[5] His case is well taken. Christian administrators who have a penchant for doing things right also have the opportunity to exercise their power with grace and humility toward creative ends. For example, a financial administrator who is responsibile for conserving resources can also apply those resources to the highest priority for achieving the purpose of the ministry. In one case, a finance officer led the way in working with a sister institution to explore and develop unified systems in computers, energy, waste management, communications, and other technical systems. The savings were applied directly to the highest priority of human services and outreach ministries.

Justice Is Our Responsibility

Third, *justice* is the special responsibility of administration. Sooner or later in the growth of any organization, the distribution of limited resources surfaces as an issue. Early in the book of Acts we read, "All of the believers were together and had everything in common. Selling their goods and possessions, they gave to anyone as he had need" (Acts 2:44–45). A short time later, we are told, "In those days when the number of disciples was increasing, the Grecian Jews among them complained against the Hebraic Jews because their widows were being overlooked in the daily distribution of food" (Acts 6:1). As a male administrator, the last thing I would ever want to do is step into the middle of the fray in which widows from Grecian and Hebraic factions are at each other's throats. Those women know how to fight. Once the sides are drawn it will take a master of diplomacy to hear the complaint, sort out the issues, and make an unbiased decision in favor of justice.

A sense of justice is a special gift for a Christian called by God for the ministry of administration. Romans 13 is usually interpreted for its

5. Crouch, *Playing God*, 7–15.

application to civic leaders who are ordained by God to exercise judgment in matters assuring the rights of citizens and protecting them from violence. Isn't the same gift at work in the administrator who makes impartial decisions in favor of justice for controversies in and beyond the faith community?

In 1974, David Hubbard, president of Fuller Theological Seminary, and I were walking through the streets of Lausanne, Switzerland, after a session of the World Conference on Evangelization. Our wandering path led us to a square where we saw the statue of Lady Justice towering over us with blindfolded eyes and an impartial balance on the scales in her hands. David, an Old Testament scholar, took one look at the sculpture and reacted, "That's not biblical justice. In the Old Testament, God does justice with his eyes wide open."

The gift of administration is not blind. After gathering all of the available facts, a Christian administrator makes a eyes-wide-open decision based upon what is morally right and impartially just. Sometimes the decision is parity, such as in the case of the seven deacons who assured equal distribution of food for the Greek and Jewish widows in Acts 6:1–7. At other times, the decision may show partiality based upon priorities, such as in the case of the poor, especially orphans and widows who have no advocate. Not everyone will agree. A good administrative decision in the cause of justice always creates an edge of controversy; otherwise there would be no need for the decision. In those moments the cohesion of the community is put to the test. Is there understanding and agreement on the purpose? Are the priorities clear? And, if push comes to shove, will love prevail? On the desk of every Christian administrator there should be the credo, "What does the Lord require of you, O man, but to love mercy, do justly, and walk humbly with your God" (Mic 6:8).

Reputation Is Our Qualification

Fourth, *reputation* is the special qualification for administration. Character is the first thought that comes to mind when we talk about the qualifications for Christian leadership. Integrity as evidenced by honesty, truthfulness, and reliability is the internal imprint of character for which we look. Reputation is character put to public test. It is what others think of you. Abraham Lincoln drew the difference between character and reputation when he said, "Character is like a tree and reputation is like a shadow. The shadow is what we think of it; the tree is the real thing."[6] While his words are wise, they do not discount the importance of Christian character being tested in the public sphere and coming out clean. According to Acts 6:3, the job qualifications for the seven deacons included the expectation that their character had already passed through the scrutiny of the public eye and come out with a "good report" among all men.

In contemporary terms, the character of the seven deacons had been "vetted" for an administrative office that bridged both secular and spiritual spheres. Not many years ago, integrity of character was assumed for candidates seeking public office. An unspoken agreement between the press and the politician covered up character faults and secret sins. Today, however, no candidate for office is exempt from scouring examination, hard-nosed assessment, and unsympathetic evaluation. The process of vetting is so rigorous that one candidate admitted, "None of us can afford to be frisked."

A good reputation earned by the acid test of character in the public sphere is still a worthy expectation for Christian administrators. Responsibility for decisions on physical, financial, legal, and human resources will inevitably involve negotiations and transactions in which the Christian administrator becomes the face of the community. The Evangelical Council for Financial Accountability was formed in the 1980s during a time when many burgeoning Christian ministries were being built on sloppy accounting and slovenly reporting. Whether in the New Testament church or the twenty-first-century evangelical movement, we need a watchdog on our reputation as well as our character.

Wisdom Is Our Need

Fifth, *wisdom* is the special need of administration. Open-eyed biblical justice assumes full perspective of the field in which the administrator makes decisions. When the seven deacons were elected to serve tables in the New Testament church, their job description required "a good reputation, practical wisdom, and being filled with the Holy Spirit" (Acts 6:3). "Practical wisdom" stands out as a gift with its roots in learning experiences over a lifetime. Wisdom itself can be theoretical and philosophical. To make that wisdom practical, however, is to bring the theory into practice and the philosophy into action. Practical wisdom is the place where the rubber meets the road.

6. Gross, *Lincoln's Own Stories*, 109.

In the early 1960s I did a research study for the president of Ohio State University on what was called the "trimester system." Academic years are typically divided into quarters or semesters. The president asked me to explore the option of dividing the academic year into three parts or trimesters in order to utilize the campus full time, year-round. As part of the study I interviewed all of the vice-presidents, deans, and directors who were in the top echelons of university administration. In every case, these administrators saw the question through the lens of their own programs. No one shared the perspective of the president, who framed the issue in the common good of the whole institution. His proposal failed because no one shared his perspective. The lesson stayed with me when I assumed a college presidency. Wise leaders are known as "big picture" people, but unless that vision touches down where practical decisions are made, it goes for naught.

Holiness Is Our Prerequisite

Sixth, *holiness or the fullness of the Spirit* is the prerequisite for administration. A good reputation and practical wisdom are necessary but not enough for selection as a Christian administrator. Each of the seven candidates for deacon in the early church knew firsthand the experience of rushing winds and tongues of fire at Pentecost. Stephen gives witness to this experience when he defends himself against the charges levied against him by the Sanhedrin. With the precision of a trial lawyer and the passion of an anointed prophet he soars beyond himself as "a man full of God's grace and power, who did great wonders and miraculous signs among the people" (Acts 6:8). Under the inspiration of the Holy Spirit, Stephen speaks with such sound reason, engaging eloquence, and spiritual understanding that even the select members of the Sanhedrin, known as the freedmen, "could not stand up against his wisdom or the spirit by which he spoke" (Acts 6:10).

An administrator who is filled with the Holy Spirit has an element of surprise for his or her witness. No one expected Stephen, a waiter of tables, to have a grasp on biblical history and God's redemptive plan in Christ that would confound theological scholars, legal experts, and government leaders. Certainly he had the background knowledge for his speech, but it took the fullness of the Holy Spirit to put it together. Christians who are called to the ministry of administration can take heart. In the midst of financial negotiations, legal tangles, and governmental regulations, opportunities will come to speak with anointing to teach and, sometimes, confound those who are caught by surprise.

Greater Good Is Our Aim

Seventh, *the greater good* is the penultimate aim of administration. Performance reviews of administrators begin with the proof of best practices in their procedures and conclude with evidence that the common good or purpose of the organization has been served by their work. In the case of the seven deacons who are elected to wait tables, the results were astounding: "So the word of God spread. The number of disciples in Jerusalem increased rapidly, and a large number of priests became obedient to the faith" (Acts 6:7). Note the double impact of breadth and depth resulting from the division of labor. As the word of God spread, it went wide as disciples increased rapidly and deep as it penetrated the ranks of the priests.

Administrators especially need the meaning that comes with a sense of partnership in achieving the purpose of the organization and the common good of the community. Leaders of managers carry this responsibility. Twice in my career as a president in Christian higher education, I had the opportunity to give special recognition to members of our administrative team. In each case, I stretched the standards for conferring honorary doctorates in the academic community. Usually, we think of honorary degrees being given to persons of esteem outside the institution whose achievements exemplify the ideals of Christian leadership. Attention also needs to be given to the unsung heroes of effective administration whose work keeps the organization running smoothly.

In the book *Boys in the Boat,* Daniel James Brown tells the story of the University of Washington men's crew winning the Olympics in 1936. Hours, days, and months of practice went into their preparation for the event. Their goal was to achieve what they called "swing," when "all eight oarsmen are rowing in such perfect union that no single action by any one is out of sync with those of all the others."[7] The analogy carries over to the role of a leader or a manager. Like a coxswain sitting in the back of the boat, the leader calls out the cadence for the race, but it is the oarsmen or managers whose discipline and coordination achieves the "swing" that synchronizes the smooth operation of the organization and gives it speed. For leaders who envision themselves standing at the bow of the boat like

7. Brown, *The Boys in the Boat,* 161–62.

George Washington crossing the Delaware and expecting the crew to do the work by image rather than instruction, the image of crew racing is a humbling experience.

A Greater Gift Is Our Bonus

Eighth, *a greater gift* is the bonus for effective administration. Stephen, the deacon, has to be the patron saint for all members of the laity whose primary task is administration. After hearing the widows' complaints, resolving the conflict over food distribution, and normalizing the procedure to assure fairness in future distributions, Stephen challenges the Sanhedrin with a sermon that parallels the Apostle Peter's masterpiece after Pentecost. After he spent three years learning at Jesus' feet and under the anointing of the Holy Spirit, we can expect such a sermon from Peter. But Stephen has the element of surprise working for him, so much so that Luke gives his words full coverage in Acts 7:1–53. No clue is given to Stephen's background. Where did he learn biblical history in such breadth? How did he grasp such depth of eternal truth? Most important of all, how did he put biblical history and eternal truth together in coherence, progression, and conclusion to give us the first, and perhaps the finest, defense of the gospel ever written? Our imagination lets us range free in search of the answer. One option is to envision Stephen being a self-taught student of the word each morning and evening before and after waiting tables. Or better yet, we can see him integrating his administrative work with the teachings of the apostles in the same way that Brother Lawrence found the opportunity for worship in kitchen work: "We can do little things for God; I turn the cake that is frying on the pan for love of him, and that done, if there is nothing else to call me, I prostrate myself in worship before him, who has given me grace to work; afterwards I rise happier than a king."[8]

Stephen may well have been transformed by a similar experience. A reputation of impeccable character, a wisdom that touched down in practice, and an experience of being filled with the Holy Spirit formed the platform from which he could be the first apologist for the Christian faith as well as the first for the church. Such spectacular spiritual and intellectual development is not a figment of the imagination. In his First Letter to Timothy, Paul says that deacons "who have served well gain an excellent standing and great assurance in their faith in Jesus Christ" (3:13). Ordained

8. Brother Lawrence, *The Practice of the Presence of God*, viii.

by the power of God, sealed by the wisdom of the Holy Spirit, and dedicated to the common good, administration is a valid, sacred, and essential calling in the package of gifts passed on from leader to leader in the process of succession.

God's Glory Is Our Goal

Ninth, the *glory of God* is the ultimate aim and end of administration. If Paul Harvey were telling us about Stephen as a faithful deacon and eloquent spokesperson for the Christian faith, he would say, "Now for the rest of the story." While teeth were gnashing and stones flying, we read, "Stephen, full of the Holy Spirit, looked up to heaven and saw the glory of God, and Jesus standing at the right hand of God. 'Look,' he said, 'I see heaven open and the Son of Man standing at the right hand of God'" (Acts 7:54–56). With this vision and these words, Stephen becomes one with Jesus in testifying, "Now this is eternal life; that they may know you, the only true God, and Jesus Christ, whom you have sent" (John 17:3). All managers who do things right also become one with Jesus and Stephen in showing the meaning of eternal life and giving the glory to God.

Whenever we think about the "work" of Jesus Christ, our thoughts go naturally to the earth-shaking events of his crucifixion and resurrection. In John 17, however, he reported that he had completed his work even before encountering the cross. We cannot forget the daily grind of Jesus going from village to village, managing details, and coaching his team. As a leader he did the right things; as manager, he did things right. The two are inseparable. Doing the right things while doing things right is a synchronized gift that every leader owes to a successor. Furthermore, in Christ's leadership, the functional never takes precedence over the relational. The gift of accomplishment passed on to our successor is spelled out, not in the achievements of our leadership, but in the evidence of maturing people who have experienced the artistry of "swing" in administration and are ready to step into the leadership role.

5

The Gift of Accountability

"I have glorified you on earth by completing the work you gave me to do."

JOHN 17:4

EVERY LEADER WANTS TO finish strong and close well. Jesus' final prayer to his Father meets these expectations when he says, "I have glorified you on earth by completing the work you gave me to do" (John 17:4). Even though his days of suffering are yet ahead, it is time to give his final report, letting the Father know that he has finished the specific task that he was called to do. He puts himself in the hands of God to be used for God's glory, even though he knows that it means humiliation, suffering, and death. Finishing strong, Jesus closes well.

Finishing Strong

Leaders choose the way they finish their careers. Some try to make up for lost time. Politicians, for instance, are notorious for overloading their final days with catch up decisions, including payoff appointments and unwarranted clemencies. At the other extreme, some leaders just let their time run out. Either from fatigue or lack of interest, they finish weak, often leaving a leadership vacuum into which self-interest rushes to create a fractious mess for the successor to clean up. Still other leaders will use the final days of their tenure to assure their legacy. In two of my successions in the presidency I inherited programs and people that could not be sustained by our resources or supported by the internal community. At a time when a new president should be casting a creative vision and anticipating affirmative decisions, I found myself resigned to personal visits with prenamed appointees for premature programs to inform them that we could not go forward with either their appointment or the program. In one case there was a threat of a lawsuit against the institution and a psychiatric examination of me based upon the analysis of my handwriting. The suit was withdrawn and the psychiatric examination was discredited. Still, the time and energy expended on the issues in the opening days of my presidencies extracted their costs.

Jesus shows us how to finish strong. In the days just prior to his final report to his Father he spent his time bringing his ministry to its conclusion. With a sense of finality in each step, Jesus left his disciples:

1. His most humble example of servanthood by washing his disciples' feet (John 13:1-6);

2. His most detailed prediction of his death and the specifics of the disciples' betrayal (John 13:18-30);

3. His most personalized promise of the Holy Spirit to comfort, teach, and empower them (John 14:15-31 and John 16:5-16);

4. His most memorable confirmation of their relationship in the analogy of the vine with the promise of fruit (John 15:1-17);

5. His most comforting words for coming persecution and mourning when grief will turn to joy (John 16:17-32); and

6. His most conclusive words of assurance in the benediction, "I have told you these things, so that in me you may have peace. In this world you will have trouble. But take heart! I have overcome the world" (John 16:33).

What more can Jesus say? With these finalities as evidence, Jesus can say to the Father, "I have completed the work that you gave me to do" (John 17:4).

The model for finishing strong is before us. To wrap up our tenure as a leader in preparation for the clean, clear cut of closure, we need to ask these questions:

• What is the example of servanthood that we want to leave?

• What are the predictions and warnings we need to share?

- What are the promises of continuity that we want to make?

- What are the truths of teaching that we want remembered?

- What words of comfort do we want to offer?

- What words of assurance do we want to include in our final benediction?

If there are any criteria for finishing strong, Jesus gives them to us with a personalized thrust that draws and challenges us.

A Timely Close

All leaders want to close well. Jesus' statement to his Father, "I have glorified you on earth by completing the work you gave me to do" (John 17:4) exudes the text and tone of closing well. His words teach us that to close well we need to leave at the *right time*. Leaders need an uncanny sense of timing, especially in reading the cues that it is time to leave. Jesus had that sense of timing. Was it supernatural or did it come from his keen perception of circumstances related to his task? At the opening of his public ministry he announced, "The time has come. The kingdom of God is near. Repent and believe the good news" (Mark 1:15). Later, in the middle of his ministry, a mob stormed the temple court where Jesus was preaching and tried to seize him, but "no one laid a hand on him because his time had not yet come" (John 7:30). Prior to washing his disciples' feet, John records, "Jesus knew that the time had come for him to leave this world and go to the Father" (John 13:1). In preparation for the Last Supper, Jesus sends his disciples out by saying, "Go into the city to a certain man and tell him, 'The Teacher says: My appointed time is near. I am going to celebrate the Passover with my disciples at your house'" (Matt 26:18). Under the shadow of the cross in Gethsemane, he concludes his final prayer and awakens the sleeping disciples with the exclamation, "Enough! The hour has come. Look, the Son of Man is betrayed into the hands of sinners. Rise! Let us go! Here comes my betrayer!" (Mark 14:41–42).

Experience as a president and a consultant to presidents tells me that the greatest temptation is to overstay our welcome. Rather than planning for succession according to the pacing and needs of the organization, the tendency is to schedule the decision on personal timing. Tragedy or despair can follow. More than once I have seen presidents plan their retirement according the magic number of twenty-five or thirty years in office. Others have tried to pressure the board into a couple more years according to their own preplanned retirement schedule. Nothing is worse than to hang around after you are no longer wanted or the community has concluded that you are no longer effective. Cases can be cited where leaders who stayed too long died early and others left with bitterness that went unhealed. After observing these cases over several decades, I often offer the advice to colleagues coming toward the end of their career, "Leave while you are loved" or "Go out on the high tide." Words of thanks have come from many friends who heeded this advice.

Jesus teaches us timing for leadership in these phases of career. There is:

a time to start;

a time to hold, and

a time to close.

His opening words in the Prayer of Succession, "Father, the time has come" (John 17:1), are spoken with resolution and finality. Having finished strong, he will close well.

A Clean Slate

Applied directly as working principles for Christian leaders who want to close well, Jesus teaches us to leave with a *clean slate*. A clean slate does not mean the loss of momentum during leadership transition. It does mean avoiding decisions that encumber the successor or leaving behind messes for the successor to clean up. For instance, during the "lame duck" period of leadership transition, incumbent officeholders are often put into the position of making decisions about starting new programs that involve a major investment of resources over an extended period of time. The drama of a start-up belongs to the incumbent, but the obligation for finishing falls to the successor. If it is possible, these initiatives should not be advanced until the successor is in place. If, however, deferral means a loss of opportunity for the organization, consultation with the successor is the order of the day. In any case, "caution" is the word about starting new initiatives and "clean" is the word for solving organizational and personnel issues.

Jesus shows us how to *close cleanly*. Leaders in transition are tempted to leave their footprints on programs and imprints on people. Special attention should be given to emotional separation from people who are appointees of the leader and loyalists who merge the personality of the leader with the vision for the mission. The results are patently unfair to successors. In extreme cases, some people never shift their loyalty to the new leader. At the extreme of extremes, loyalists even persist as a subversive unit engaged in sabotaging the new leader. To avoid these unnecessary complications, a leader should separate from the organization and its people, not just by position, but also by emotional and even physical distance.

Jesus again shows us the way. Right up front, he tells his disciples that he must go away and they will not see him again. With the loss of his physical presence they will also lose his psychological, sociological, and spiritual support. Into the gap of separation Jesus promises the presence of the Holy Spirit to continue as the one who walks alongside them, teaches them on the way, empowers them for their task, and comforts them in crisis. What more can Jesus say or do? He has finished his task, nurtured his followers, commended his successor, envisioned the future, and glorified God.

What if we applied these criteria for closing well to our leadership? In reflective moments I have looked back upon three successions in the presidency and asked if I, according to Jesus' example, closed well. In each case, I finished the task given to me: developing a fully-accredited Christian liberal arts institution at Spring Arbor College (now University); turning around a financial crisis and advancing to university status at Seattle Pacific College; and resourcing the vision of world Wesleyan leadership at Asbury Theological Seminary. With confidence, I can say that each of my successors inherited a viable and sustainable organization with a clear mission and limited encumbrances. As best I can ascertain, I tried to give the glory to God. Whether my colleagues in the institutions where I served would agree or disagree is the more fundamental question. In Jesus' case, his colleagues and more than 2,000 years of history confirm that he finished strong and closed well. History will also be my judge.

The Age of Accountability

Accountability is the affirmation of faithfulness. Jesus finished strong and closed well because he was accountable to the Father for the authority he was given, the task to which he was assigned, and the people who were entrusted to him. Without accountability we cannot finish strong or close well.

I first heard the phrase "the age of accountability" when I was an eight-year-old boy sitting under the convicting ministry of a "hellfire-and-brimstone" evangelist. Extrapolating his doctrine of accountability from Jesus' first visit to the temple, the fiery preacher told us that we became accountable for our sins at the age of twelve. A sigh of relief passed through me as the guilt of my childhood transgressions was temporarily lifted and I anticipated four more years of blissful sinning before I would become accountable. Not by coincidence, I was converted at the age of twelve.

A similar situation existed in our society one or two generations ago. Public confidence in our leaders and our institutions permitted them to serve without accountability except in cases of gross malfeasance. All that has changed today. Accountability has come of age as public confidence in our leaders and our institutions has turned into doubt and distrust. John Kennedy, for instance, never had to account for his trysts with Marilyn Monroe in the bedroom of the White House, but Bill Clinton has had every filthy detail of his liaison with Monica Lewinsky aired in the media. Sixty years ago no one had to account for the death of 759 American soldiers and sailors who were killed by German torpedo boats off the coast of England during the final practice for the D-Day landing because of the failure of military intelligence. Today, the terrorist assault on our embassy in Benghazi and assassination of four Americans is a specter of shame that will not go away. Millions of dollars and months of time have gone into the investigation to determine who is accountable.

Although accountability has come of age, it is not new. From the beginning to the end of Scripture, the wheel of accountability turns. Genesis opens with God himself accounting for the quality of his creative work and pronouncing it "very good" (Gen 1:31). Revelation closes with the standard of accounting that no one shall add or subtract from the word of God without his or her name being erased from the Book of Life (Rev 22:18–19). In between Genesis and Revelation is the repeated truth of human accountability to God and in relationship to other people. Accountability rings from the ethical peak of the Old Testament when Micah speaks, "He has showed you, O man, what is good. And what does the Lord require of you? To act justly and to love mercy and to walk humbly with your God" (Mic 6:8). Accountability breathes in every word when Jesus sums up the Law and the prophets in the simple sentences, "Love the Lord your God with all your heart and with all your soul and with all your mind. This is the first and greatest commandment. And the second is like it: Love your neighbor as yourself" (Matt 22:37–39). We should not be surprised, then, to read that Jesus gives an accountability report when he finishes the work that the Father gave him to do.

As the Prayer of Succession continues through John 17, the agenda of accountability that Jesus accepts unfolds before us. In chapter 2 we learned how Jesus accounts for the exercise of authority entrusted to him. Now as the Prayer of Succession advances, we see how Jesus also accepts responsibility for:

- the task he is assigned to do;
- the word he speaks;
- the name he bears;
- the tone he sets;
- the example he gives;
- the hope he sees;
- the unity he knows;
- the love he shares.

In one way or another every Christian leader shares these responsibilities and the accountability that goes with them.

The Test of Accountability

Over a career in Christian higher education that spanned forty-one years as a professor, dean, vice-president, and president, institutions where I served went through scores of examining visits from state, regional, and national accrediting agencies. Following these visits we received a detailed report on the findings of the committee. In support of the decision to grant or deny accreditation, the report listed both strengths and weaknesses found by the examining team. For our strengths, there were commendations. For our weaknesses, there were suggestions, recommendations, and notations. A suggestion was a gentle nudge to correct a minor weakness; a recommendation was a more specific proposal for improvement; but a notation was a requirement for change, including a follow-up report. If the notations were not heeded, the accreditors could actually put the institution on a "show cause" notice with the threat of losing recognition in the academic community.

In the book of Revelation, Jesus actually becomes the examiner for accrediting the seven churches of Asia. After visiting those churches, he issues a written report evaluating their strengths and weaknesses. For their strengths, Jesus has commendations. For their weaknesses, he has suggestions, recommendations, notations, and even "show cause" notices. In summarizing his visit, Jesus says that if they heed his report, they will receive the crown of life. But if they ignore his warnings, he will remove their candlestick from the golden lampstand at his right hand.

Assume that you were visited by Christ at the time when you were ready to hand over leadership to your successor. Assume that he examines you on each of the standards of accountability which he held for himself. How would you answer these questions:

Have I glorified God with the authority entrusted to me?

Have I finished the work that God called me to do?

Have I effectively spoken the word of truth?

Have I been true to the name I bear?

Have I seen joy in those who follow me?

Have I empowered others to be holy by the example I set?

Have I cast a vision of hope for sustaining the movement?

Have I shown my oneness with Christ and the Father?

Have I demonstrated the sacrificial love that is witness to my faith?

Even now the Spirit of God may be nudging you with suggestions for change, impressing on you specific recommendations for improvement, putting you on notations that demand immediate and radical action, or even sounding the warning of a "show cause" notice to change your name or change your character. As the final step in finishing strong and closing well, we must be accountable for every dimension of our leadership. If we can we pray to the Father with the confidence of Jesus, "I have brought you glory on earth by completing the work you gave me to do," our successor will receive a gift of inestimable worth—the gift of accountability that is wrapped in the gold foil of finishing strong and tied with the blue ribbon of closing well.

PART II

The Legacy of Truth

6

The Gift of Acceptance

"For I gave them the words you gave me and they accepted them."

JOHN 17:8

HOW DO YOU PREPARE twelve common men in a short course of three-and-a-half years to lead a world movement? The question barely scratches the surface of the challenge faced by Jesus Christ. All of the odds are stacked against him—unlearned students, limited time, religious opposition, and a hostile environment. Only one teaching resource will give him a chance. It is the word of truth spoken to him by the Father that he must speak and his disciples must make their own.

A teacher is naturally motivated by this challenge. If the word of truth received from the Father and taught by the Son can be fully believed, embraced, and enacted, the results will be a leadership team ready to change the world. Jesus will have given to them the greatest gift of succession in human history, a personal relationship with the transforming word of truth as their legacy for leadership. Rather than rushing to accept this conclusion as inevitable, however, there are probing questions that need to be answered. A teacher will immediately see a full curriculum between the text of his teaching—the "words you gave me"—and the test of his teaching: "they accepted them" (John 17:8). What is the word of truth that the Father has entrusted to his Son? What went on between the "giving" of the word to Jesus and the "accepting" of the word by his disciples? What does it mean when it says that Jesus' disciples "accepted" them? If we can answer these questions about Jesus' accountability for the word of truth with application to our own leadership, we will add another dimension to our legacy and another gift for our successor.

The Word of Truth

Jesus has already given an accountability report to the Father on the authority entrusted to him. True to the Father's trust, he used that authority to complete the task of bringing eternal life to all people and glorifying God. Now, in the words, "For I gave them the words you gave me . . ." (John 17:8a), Jesus adds accountability for the word of truth that the Father has personally spoken and entrusted to him.

The Infinite Word

Jesus' accountability report on the word of truth entrusted to him has to be framed within the monumental declaration opening John's Gospel, "In the beginning was the Word, and the Word was with God, and the Word was God. He was with God in the beginning. Through him all things were made; without him nothing was made that has been made. In him was life, and that life was the light of men" (John 1:1–4). What more can be said? Jesus is the eternal Word, the author of creation, and the light of the world. Yet, in accounting for the words that the Father gave him, he makes no claim on first authorship. In fact, he goes out of his way to disclaim authorship: "These words you hear are not my own; they belong to the Father who sent me" (John 14:24).

The Incarnate Word

Our lesson in humility continues as John takes us down, down, down from the infinite Word to the incarnate Word when he is inspired to write, "The Word became flesh and made his dwelling among us. We have seen his glory, the glory of the One and Only, who came from the Father, full of grace and truth" (John 1:14). Platonic reasoning says that the pure Word could not be contaminated by the impurities of the flesh or the corruption of society. Yet, in the incarnation Jesus took that chance because a person-to-person relationship was the only way to prepare his disciples as his successors for continuing the redemptive mission.

The Living Word

John then proceeds to write the story of the Word as it unfolds in the life of Jesus Christ. From the lips of Jesus himself, we learn the meaning of the Word with which he has been entrusted. Early on, he tells his grumbling disciples that his words are more than human words. "The Spirit gives life; the flesh counts for nothing. The words I have spoken to you are spirit and they are life" (John 6:63). Shortly thereafter, Jesus draws out from Peter an insight that extends this truth to its eternal dimensions. He does this by asking his disciples if they will also leave him because of the hard facts related to his death. Peter confesses for all, "Lord, to whom shall we go? You have the word of eternal life" (John 6:68). Later on, as Jesus' enemies close in, he intensifies his teaching about the meaning of his words. He speaks of the indwelling Word: "If anyone loves me, he will obey my teaching. My Father will love him, and we will come to him and make our home with him" (John 14:23). He speaks of the cleansing Word. In the parable of the vine and the branches, when Jesus talks about pruning, he reminds his disciples, "You are already clean because of the word I have spoken to you" (John 15:3). As a natural follow-up to the cleansing Word, Jesus gives them the promising Word: "If you remain in me and my word remains in you, ask whatever you wish, and it will be given you" (John 15:7).

The Intouchable Word

Through the infinite Word, we see the light and know God; through the incarnate Word we see his grace and truth in order to believe; and through the living Word we receive eternal life. While knowing, believing, and living the word of truth are essential steps in the disciples' journey of faith, are they sufficient preparation for the succession of leadership after Jesus returns to the Father? John, in his First Epistle, gives us insight into another dimension of the word of truth when he writes, "That which was from the beginning, which we have heard, which we have seen with our eyes, which we have looked at and our hands have touched—this we proclaim concerning the Word of life" (1 John 1:1). Here is the key to Jesus' preparation of his disciples for succession. To borrow a newly coined term from the media world, John is talking about the intouchable Word, meaning an intimate relationship with truth and hands-on teaching in real time. (*Intouchable* is the title of a French movie telling the story of Driss, who is a reluctant caregiver with a criminal background. He provides care for Phillippe, a super-wealthy man who became a quadriplegic due to a paragliding accident. Rather than compounding pity for his charge, Driss challenges Phillippe to take risks, including revealing his handicap to Eleonore, a lover by letter and phone. In the end, Driss sets up his final challenge by arranging a surprise luncheon at which he will suddenly disappear and Eleonore will arrive to meet Phillippe face to face for the first time. Driss is then seen walking away and waving with the tacit understanding that love will now have a chance.)

Until a leader is willing to make the sacrificial investment in those who are entrusted to her or him, change will be small and growth will be minimal. For Jesus this means time, energy, and patience with disciples who are unlearned, shortsighted, and frequent failures. Yet, because they hear him personally, see him constantly, and touch him frequently, the message gets through. John goes on to announce the outcome of Jesus' teaching: "We proclaim to you what we have seen and heard, so that you also may have fellowship with us. And our fellowship is with the Father and with his Son, Jesus Christ" (1 John 1:3). In these words we learn what Jesus means when he says, "For I gave them the words you gave me and they accepted them" (John 17:6).

"Accepted" is too passive a term to describe either Jesus' teaching method or the disciples' learning experience. Eugene Peterson captures the full-orbed sense of acceptance when he writes in *The Message*, "And they took it and were convinced that I came from you. They believed that you had sent me" (John 17:8). Three levels of learning depth are seen in these words. At the cognitive level of learning they "*took*" the Word; at the volitional level they were "*convinced*" by it; and at the affective level they "*believed.*" Jesus is reporting that his relational teaching with the disciples has resulted in the full scope of sound learning. As the Father's Word is the Son's Word, the Son's Word in now the disciples' Word. Jesus can look back upon the teaching-learning experience with his disciples and report this outcome to his Father: "All I have is yours, and all you have is mine. And glory has come to me through them" (John 17:10).

John concludes his Gospel with his own understanding of the words of Jesus Christ. He writes, "Jesus did many other miraculous signs in the presence of his disciples, which are not recorded in this book. These are written that you may believe that Jesus is the Christ, the Son of God, and that by believing you may have life in his name" (John 20:31). The loop is closed. In the opening words of the Prayer of Succession Jesus accepts the authority given to him by his Father "that he might give eternal life to all those you have given him. Now, this is eternal life: that they may know you, the only true God and Jesus Christ whom you have sent" (John 17:2–3). In the closing words of his Gospel, then, John witnesses to the fact that Jesus has been true to his trust, effectively communicating the words of the Father so that all those who accept them will believe that he is Jesus Christ, the Son and God, and in believing, they will have eternal life.

The God-Breathed Process

To bring his disciples to a holistic and mature level of learning, Jesus employs the methods of a master teacher. In teaching the word of truth to the disciples as individuals, Jesus uses the same method that is seen in the model for "God-breathed" teaching through the Word in 2 Timothy 3:16–17. Jesus employs all four types of instruction identified in the passage with his disciples: (1) *teaching* truth; (2) *rebuking* error; (3) *correcting* deviation; and (4) *training* in righteousness. John Stott tells us that the first two steps teach creed; the second two steps teach conduct.[1] In each of these two sets of teaching tools we see positive and negative learning. For our creed, the "God-breathed" Word teaches us true doctrine and negatively reproves false doctrine. For our conduct as well, negative teaching corrects wrong behavior at the same time that positive teaching trains us in righteousness. With his uncanny gift for making truth clear, Stott sums up the outcomes for these teaching tools: "For the creed, or what we believe, the Spirit teaches us to overcome error and grow in truth; for our conduct, or how we behave, the Spirit teaches us to overcome evil and grow in holiness."[2]

Paul, then, presents his gift of succession to Timothy, called to be a Christian leader in a pluralistic and permissive age. He writes, "so that the man of God may be thoroughly equipped for every good work" (2 Tim 3:17). Through the teaching of the "God-breathed" Word, Timothy is urged by Paul, his teacher, to "stand firm" against pressure to dilute the truth, against the temptation to compromise on moral standards, and, if

1. Stott, *The Message of 2 Timothy*, 103.

2. Ibid.

necessary, to stand alone. Jesus has the same purpose in his "tell and show, touch and see" teaching of the Word to his disciples. With each of his disciples becoming "a whole man of God thoroughly equipped for every good work," the disciple is being prepared to lead in a hostile world, standing firm, and if necessary, standing alone for the word of truth (2 Tim 3:17). The disciples' maturity as leaders is now readied for the crowning moment when the Holy Spirit will bring "all truth" to their remembrance and "all power" to their potential.

In the mirror of Jesus' teaching, I see my weakness as a Christian leader. Early on in my career I put a premium upon appointing the best and the brightest to my executive team and then giving them free rein to run with their gifts. To the credit of these colleagues, they grew on their own and performed well. Not until my third presidency did I get serious about growth plans for the executives who served with me. I asked each one to prepare a professional and personal growth plan that we would share and I would resource. Again, the demands of the presidency took the keen edge off these plans, but nevertheless, I learned the value of meeting regularly with my direct reports, hearing of their progress, and helping them take their next steps.

When I am asked what I would do differently if I could rerun my years in a presidency, it becomes clear that I would give more attention to planning, resourcing, and following the development of those who led with me. Especially, I would center the plans for leadership development around the teaching of the word. To begin, I would ask that we unconditionally accept the word of truth as the text for our teaching. Next, I would give more attention to a self-giving and sharing relationship around the word of truth with my direct reports. Then, I would accept responsibility for the outcome of our teaching-learning relationship with the goal of being able to say with Jesus, "For I have given them the words that you gave me and they accepted them" (John 17:8). A legacy of eternal truth, relational teaching, and maturing disciples makes up another gift of succession to those who follow us.

Commencement Time

I think I know how Jesus felt when he presented his disciples to the Father in the Prayer of Succession. For thirty-three consecutive years I presided at college, university, and seminary commencements. As president it was my privilege to confer the degrees upon the graduating students. Prior to awarding the degrees I spoke the solemn words, "According to the authority vested in me by the board of trustees, and on recommendation of the faculty, I hereby confer upon you the appropriate degree with all of the rights, privileges, and responsibilities pertaining thereto." Joyful moments followed as the graduates came forward one by one to receive their diplomas, shake my hand, and turn the tassel on their caps from left to right. At the end, all of the family, friends, and witnesses in the audience stood, clapped, and cheered as the graduates threw their caps into the air. The glory belonged to the faculty, but as president I beamed with the knowledge that another generation of graduates had been prepared to advance the cause of Christ in a needy world.

Jesus must have felt the same way about his disciples as he presented them to his Father. We can almost hear him saying, "According to the authority vested in me by my Father, and on recommendation of his Spirit, I hereby confer upon you the honor of being my apostles for the word of truth, with all of the rights, privileges, and responsibilities pertaining thereto." Project that same image forward to the time of transition for your own leadership. Will you be able to present followers to your successor, who has accepted the word of truth as their own and is ready to communicate it to others? Highest honors go with the gift of acceptance.

7

The Gift of Assurance

"Holy Father, protect them by the power
of your name—the name you gave me—
so that they may be one even as we are one."

(JOHN 17:11B)

WITH AUTHORITY GIVEN BY Christ and maturity taught by his word, the apostles are ready for a real-time test. Jesus is going to leave them to continue his work in a hostile and hateful world. He knows from personal experience what they will face in this high-risk environment. Hostility will come in the evil one's targeted attacks against their faith and hatred will come from leaders and people who reject their message and undermine their hope. What assurance can Jesus give them as he lets them go? His prayer is simple. He asks that the Father give his successors the protection of his name and the fullness of his joy. Jesus counts on these two promises to assure the continuing oneness of the disciples with himself and his Father. The risk is high and the results are uncertain. Once again, we have to be willing to bet that Christ is right.

The Art of Letting Go

Every teacher knows the pain of letting students go, especially when they are cast into a hostile environment with unproven skills and without the teacher's immediate presence. Baby birds know the experience when the mother bird pushes them out of the nest with the tweet, "Fly or else." As cruel as it seems, there is a critical time for teachers, mentors, and mother birds to let go. The natural tendency is to hold their charges back as long as possible.

As an observer of teaching and mentoring relationships, I have concluded that the timing for the release of a student or a protégé is a test of leadership. When a teacher or mentor refuses to set his/her followers free, the relationship coagulates into codependency that is detrimental to both parties. Both begin to depend upon the other for ego strength and both stop growing. A cultic climate is created and the participants become dysfunctional malcontents in the organization. As I remember individuals or groups of individuals who caused me grief in leadership, they shared one factor in common. Not only had they stopped growing, but they had no place to go. With their options closed they turned back within themselves to become saboteurs in the system. These observations led me to be a champion for options in the personal and professional development plans of the persons whom I was called to lead. When they came to me with word of other offers, I said, "I really don't want the people whom no else wants. Let's talk about options. If I can't offer you an option for growth, I will urge you to go where you can grow." At times it meant the possibility of losing good people with high potential, but I am convinced that "letting go" in timely fashion is one of the hard decisions that a leader is called to make.

Jesus made that hard decision when he had to let his disciples go. Yes, the decision was forced by the impending threat of his arrest. Yes, the risk of letting them go was tempered by the promise of his presence in the coming of the Holy Spirit. Still, the decision had to be difficult. One can feel the pathos in Jesus' prayer, "Holy Father, protect them by the power of your name—the name you gave me—so that they may be one even as we are one" (John 17:11). The fact that he asks for their protection by the power of the Holy Father's name is enough to tell us that he was not making an easy decision. He does not want to leave them unprotected in a hostile world where the hatred against him will be turned against them. He does not want to let them go before they are ready. Yet, he has no choice. The Father's timing is his timing, and his timing is the disciples' timing. With complete confidence in the power of the Father's name, he lets them go.

The Protection of His Name

What's in a name? Jesus is pleading with his Holy Father for the power of his name to protect his disciples and keep them bonded together as one in love. Not by coincidence, Jesus invokes the Name "Holy Father" in his prayer. By appealing to God's formal name, Jesus is asking for the protection of his sovereignty as well as his compassion. His sovereignty will set limits on what the evil one can do to those who are at one with him and who carry his name. Young adults of today would give the protection of God's sovereignty special meaning by saying, "He's got your back." Isaiah gave the same assurance to the Israelites on their way home to Jerusalem from their Babylonian exile, "for the Lord will go before you, the God of Israel will be your rear guard" (Isa 52:12). Jesus experienced the attacks of Satan from both front and flank. In the face-to-face confrontation in the wilderness, he had countered Satan's temptation with the word of God. But in moments of flattery, such as when the crowd wanted to make him king or the Greeks wanted an audience with him, he retreated into the protection of the will of God.

Jesus also prayed for the compassion of the Father in protecting his disciples. The image of a shepherd comes forward. During his time with the disciples Jesus identified himself as the Good Shepherd. In close connection with his final prayer, Jesus had said, "I am the good shepherd: I know my sheep and my sheep know me—just as the Father knows me and I know the Father—I lay down my life for the sheep" (John 10:14–15). Usually we think of the shepherd leading his sheep to greener pastures, but in this context, Jesus is talking about protecting them from the stealthy attack of a wolf, even at the cost of his own life. Sheep also need protection from their own impetuous nature, blind obedience, and frequent stupidity. Earlier in the same chapter, Jesus describes himself as the watchman who "calls his own sheep by name and leads them out. When he has brought out all his own, he goes on ahead of them, and his sheep follow him because they know his voice" (John 10:3–4). Peter would learn about that kind of protective care when Jesus said to him in the garden of Gethsemane, "Simon, Simon, Satan has asked to sift you as wheat. But I have prayed for you, Simon, that your faith may not fail. And when you have turned back, strengthen your brothers" (John 10:31–32). Even though Peter went through denial of his Lord with deepest shame, the shepherding care of Jesus did not fail. The Gospel of John closes with the commissioning of Peter to be the shepherd of the sheep just as Jesus had led and protected him.

Twofold protection in the name of the Holy Father is still needed. We cannot survive without the assurance that God's will sets limits for Satan's attacks and that his compassion covers our weaknesses so that we remain one with Father and Son.

The Power of His Name

The scene shifts dramatically when Jesus joins the Father in protecting his disciples by "the name you gave me" (John 17:11). When push comes to shove, it is the name of Jesus Christ, the Son of God, that draws the line and defines the difference for both hatred and protection in a hostile world. Return to John's final words in his Gospel: "But these are written that you may believe that Jesus is the Christ, the Son of God, and that by believing you may have life in his name" (John 20:31). There is no equivocation in these words. We must confess the full name of Jesus Christ as the Son of God if we are to have eternal life. Paul raised that personal confession to its ultimate level when he wrote, "Therefore God exalted him to the highest place and gave him the name that is above every name, that at the name of Jesus every knee should bow, in heaven and on earth and under the earth, and every tongue confess that Jesus Christ is Lord, to the glory of God the Father" (Phil 2:9–11).

Despite the clarity of Scripture, controversy over the deity of Christ has continued to be a threat to the unity of the church. In 326 AD Constantine called the Council of Nicea to resolve the issue. With the shift of a single letter in the noun describing the nature of Christ, Arius destroyed the unity of the Godhead by contending that the Son was a created being and unequal with the Father. Athanasius, his opponent, refuted this claim by affirming that the Son was truly God, coeternal with the Father and at one with him. After extended debate, the council voted for the adoption of the Nicene Creed, the same creed that defines Christian orthodoxy and the creed that we recite today:

> I believe in one God: the Father Almighty, maker of heaven and earth, and of all things visible and invisible;
>
> And in one Lord Jesus Christ, the only begotten Son of God: begotten of the Father before all worlds, God of God, Light of Light, very God of very God, begotten, not made, being of one substance with the Father, through whom all things were made; who for us

men and for our salvation came down from heaven, and was incarnate by the Holy Ghost of the Virgin Mary, and was made man, and was crucified also for us under Pontius Pilate; he suffered and was buried, and the third day he rose again according to the Scriptures, and ascended into heaven, and sitteth on the right hand of the Father, and he shall come again with glory, to judge both the quick and the dead; whose kingdom shall have no end.

Notable is the fact that separate and complete sentences define the Father and the Son. The holy conjunction of "and" then joins "one God, the Father almighty," and "one Lord Jesus Christ, the only begotten Son of God." Anything short of this confession cannot qualify as Christian faith.

Yet, in every generation since the Council of Nicea, the name of the Lord Jesus Christ, the Son of God, has been called into question. Today, we can point to biblical scholars who use higher criticism of the Scriptures in order to justify their search for the historic, not the Nicean, Jesus. Interest in the subject spills over into best sellers in both fiction and non-fiction. In 2013 a book titled *The Zealot* rose to the top of the New York Times best sellers in the nonfiction category. Reza Aslan, a student of religious history and a professor of creative writing, combined his areas of specialization to author a knowledgeable and well-written book around the premise that the only truth we know about Jesus is that he lived and that he died. Everything else is a matter of faith in a story concocting that he is Jesus Christ, Son of God. In the end Aslan proclaims faith in Jesus, a son of man.[1] To come to that conclusion, however, he relies on the Scriptures to carry his case against the Scriptures. Christian readers are perturbed by his attack, and in response, non-Christian readers are rallying to his cause. If history repeats itself, Aslan's book will join the list of best-selling forgettables while the story of the other Aslan written by C. S. Lewis will continue to top the list.

Questioning the name of Jesus Christ, the Son of God, is not limited to scholars, journalists, and media makers outside the faith. Attempts to be relevant or edgy as a way of communicating with a generation that is questioning the institutional church and the gospel it represents has often led to dilution of the name of Jesus Christ. Cars and buses in Seattle are carrying the sticker that reads "Jesus is _____." To the credit of its creators from a local megachurch, the sticker prompts the reader's attention to the name and meaning of Jesus. But, with the option to fill in the blank as the reader might choose, the sticker plays into the hands of those who want to make

---

1. Aslan, *The Zealot*, 216.

Jesus in their own image. According to Scripture, the only name that can fill in the blank is "Lord," meaning that he is Christ, the Son of God.

In a similar vein, there are popular movements within evangelical Christianity that are trying to respond to younger people who claim to be spiritual without being religious. More than likely, they also claim to like Jesus as their loving friend but not as their sovereign Lord. The entry point into many megachurch ministries begins with some human hurt with which Jesus' compassion is identified. Nothing is wrong with this except that the ministry never advances to the hard truths of the gospel, namely the reality of sin, the price of the cross, the power of the resurrection, and the recognition that only Jesus Christ, the Son of God, can redeem us.

The Holy Name

So again, what's in a name? From the Prayer of Succession we learn that the name of the Holy Father is our protector and in oneness with the name of Jesus Christ, the Son of God, our Lord and Savior. When Jesus prays, "may they be one as we are one" (John 17:21) he invites us to take his name. To the credit of the people of Antioch, known for creating names consistent with a movement among them, "The disciples were first called Christians at Antioch" (Acts 11:26). The name was based on evidence. The name "Christian" was consistent with what they believed and to whom they belonged.

Try as we might, the name "Christian" cannot be diluted or substituted. As the contest of world religions intensifies and the secular mind-set penetrates the ranks of the faithful, to carry the name "Christian" will not be nominal or cultural—it will be creedal and communal. As persecuted people around the world can testify, to take the name "Christian" identifies what we believe and to whom we belong. It also defines our character and our conduct. Jesus prayed that his disciples might be holy as well as protected. For good reason he addressed the Father as "Holy" and prayed that he and his disciples might be one with the Father in purity of character and consistency of conduct. His challenge, "Be holy as I am holy" (1 Peter 1:16) is not nullified by our attempts to sidestep the question or debate its meaning. To be identified with the name of Jesus Christ, the Son of God, is to be drawn by an insatiable thirst to be holy as he is holy in both character and conduct.

Although I have never suffered for the name of Jesus Christ, I got a taste of a hostile environment when, as president of Seattle Pacific University, I offered the invocation at the Seattle Rotary Club. I closed my prayer, "In the Name of Jesus Christ we pray. Amen." A minor firestorm followed when a prominent civic leader from the Jewish community personally confronted me on the prayer. We were friends and respected each other, but he insisted that I offended non-Christian members with my closing words. A long conversation followed in which I took the position that the invocation should be given by persons of different religious traditions with the freedom to pray according to the character and convictions of their faith position. Then I said, "I am sorry if I offended you. I must pray in Jesus' name because that is who I am." We parted friends, an informal policy of freedom in diversity was adopted, and there was no rebuttal the next time I prayed in Jesus' name.

Oneness with the name of the Father was the legacy for which Jesus prayed and the gift of succession that he left for his disciples. With the same oneness, he left us his name as our legacy. Christian leaders today are under equal obligation to assure the oneness of his name as our gift of succession for our followers. Whenever the mantle of leadership is passed from one Christian leader to another, the question must be asked, *"Is the name of Jesus Christ, Son of God, the legacy of our leadership, that identifies us, protects us, and makes us one with the will of the Holy Father?"* All other gifts of succession depend on an affirmative answer to this question.

8

The Gift of Affirmation

"I am coming to you now, but I say these things
while I am still in the world, so that they may
have the full measure of my joy within them"

(JOHN 17:13)

JESUS DOES NOT MINCE words. Brutal reality awaits his disciples after he leaves them. They will face the same personal hatred and social hostility that their Lord faced. Only two guarantees are given. As they go into the world without him, Jesus prays that they will be protected from the evil one by the power of the Father's name and that as they suffer they will experience the full measure of Christ's joy, both assured by the presence of the Holy Spirit.

Something is wrong. Suffering and joy are complete opposites. Suffering is a condition created by circumstances that test body, mind, and soul. Joy is a spirit of exuberant gratitude that is independent of circumstances. The paradox defies human understanding. We tend to come down on one side or the other. Of course, we prefer joy to suffering. For years now I have signed my letters and emails with the valediction, "With His joy." Yes, I consider myself a joyful spirit because of the presence of Christ, but after confronting the paradox of suffering and joy, I wonder if I am sending a message that becomes flippant if overused. Whenever I meet Christians who have been persecuted for their faith in other countries I marvel at the full measure of joy that I see in them. After reading Jesus' prayer and understanding the paradox of joy, I have chosen to sign off on my communication more frequently with the words, "Only by His grace." I still have joy but I am reluctant to claim its fullness because of the limits of my suffering.

To focus on either extreme of suffering or joy is to put a blight on our Christian faith. Suffering can lead to religious paranoia and joy can be a giddy form of the prosperity gospel. Only as we grasp the meaning of eternal truth can the paradox be resolved. As we know good because of evil, truth because of falsehood, and beauty because of ugliness, we know the fullness of joy because of suffering.

Jesus, of course, leads the way in resolving the paradox. Whenever we think about the combination of suffering and joy in the life of Jesus we immediately go to Hebrews 12:2 and the words slip so easily off our tongue, "Let us fix our eyes on Jesus, the author and perfecter of our faith, who for the joy set before him endured the cross, scorning its shame, and sat down at the right hand of the throne of God." As true as these words are, it is hard to identify with Jesus in the crucifixion and endure his suffering for the sake of future joy. They tell us more about Jesus than they do about us. After reading them, we want to worship him rather than assume that we can enter into the fellowship of his sufferings.

Jesus understands our dilemma. He does not dodge the issue. Very personally and with unmistakable intent he prays that his disciples "may have the full measure of my joy within them" (John 17:13). What is meant by the "full measure" of Christ's joy? A search through Scripture leads us toward the answer. In his own words as well as through the words of New Testament writers, we see a composite picture of what Jesus means by the full measure of his joy. In every case, there is a link between a need that is suffered and the exuberant note of joy that follows when the need is met. Let the experience of Jesus speak for itself.

The Joy of Simple Faith

In what did Jesus find the fullness of joy? We will be surprised by the answer because it is so contrary to our typical quest for joy. While we bow and scrape for the joy of recognition by preachers, politicos, professors, and pundits, Luke tells us, "At that time Jesus, full of joy through the Holy Spirit, said, 'I praise you, Father, Lord of heaven and earth, because you have hidden these things from the wise and learned, and revealed them to little children. Yes, Father, for this was your good pleasure'" (Luke 10:21). After a lifetime in academia as a professor, dean, and president, I know what Jesus means. While there is no doubt about the faith of the "wise and the learned" who profess Christ, there is also the expectation they will be reserved in their expression of joy. Going another step, the sense of joy can give way to the notion that intellectuals have to be skeptical. Remember the budding scholar who said, "I wanted to be a philosopher, but cheerfulness kept creeping in." Great joy, however, attends the intellectual who can speak the simple language of faith at the same time that he or she can probe deeply into its dilemmas. Paul, who could claim "eloquence and superior wisdom" based upon academic credentials, wrote, "My message and my preaching were not with wise and persuasive words, but with a demonstration of the Spirit's power, so that your faith might not rest on men's wisdom, but on God's power" (1 Cor 2:4–5). In our generation we have seen this demonstration of God's power expressed with joy in such leaders as John Stott, Dallas Willard, Eugene Peterson, Os Guinness, Richard Foster, Elizabeth Elliott, Calvin Miller, Bill Pannell, Arthur Holmes, Ray Bakke, Martin Marty, Howard Snyder, Frank Gaberlein, Rick Warren, Rebecca Manley Pippert, Vernon Grounds, and others. In each case, their joy bubbled up in a playful, childlike way. John Stott, for instance, started a lecture at Asbury Theological Seminary by taking a drink of water. As he wiped his lips he said that it reminded him of the Anglican priest who always took a glass of milk into the pulpit. One day some pranksters spiked the milk with brandy. When the priest interrupted his sermon to take a sip of milk, he licked his lips and remarked, "Umm, that must have been some cow." Stott then went on to preach one of his sermons blending profound wisdom with simple faith. Needless to say, his words were "full of joy through the Holy Spirit" (Luke 10:21).

The Joy of Just One

Whenever we study the Bible we want to pay particular attention to the amount of space that is given to a subject. Following that principle we note that Jesus told three parables in a row about the priority of his love for just one lost soul, whether represented by a sheep, a coin, or a prodigal son. In each case, recovery led to joy. The shepherd who found the lost sheep and the woman who found her lost coin called in their friends and neighbors to rejoice with them and, of course, the father who found his lost son threw a banquet.

Immediately after our marriage in 1950, my wife, Jan, and I received a one-year appointment to a small pastorate in Vicksburg, Michigan while I completed my bachelor's degree at Western Michigan University. A parish with thirty members that paid thirty-five dollars a week welcomed us even though the average age of the membership was in the high sixties (or so it seemed) while I was twenty-one and Jan was nineteen. In the short period of two months Jan went from a college cheerleader to "Sister McKenna," head of the Women's Missionary Society. It was a good year preaching twice on Sundays, leading prayer meetings on Wednesdays, working with high school youth, and making pastoral calls on every member. The highlight, however, was our evangelistic effort with a young couple around the corner who had the luxury of a television set and invited us to watch it with them. During the year they faced some rocky moments in their marriage and we helped keep them together with our friendship. No overt witness was needed. They knew that we were just kids with pastoral identification. But, as the year went by, we began to pray that the Lord would help lead them to saving faith before I graduated from college and we moved on to seminary. Of course, we had invited them to church from time to time, but without success. One Sunday late in the year, however, they surprised us by coming to the Sunday morning service. Our prayers intensified and they came back for two more Sundays. Now, in the simplest of faith, we asked the Holy Spirit to bring them to faith as the crowning moment for our year's ministry. Two Sundays later, after I preached, Dick stepped from his seat and came to the altar. Fran immediately followed. Tears of joy flooded our eyes and flowed down our cheeks as Jan and I wrapped our arms around them and heard them ask forgiveness of God and each other. Like the prodigal son coming home, the woman finding the lost coin, and the merchant finding the pearl of great price, we discovered the joy that can be known only when the lost is found.

The Joy of Forgotten Pain

There is no joy in pain—especially when it is the pain of death. As I write this, our neighbors, Don and Carol James, are going through the most excruciating pain. Don, the legendary College Football Hall of Fame coach for the University of Washington, has just been sent home with hospice care as he suffers through the final stages of fast-acting pancreatic cancer. His family is taking turns to assure a round-the-clock presence during his dying hours. To meet them in the hall is to see beautiful Christian people devastated by the harsh reality of pain and the exhaustion of sleepless nights. Great grief is just ahead, even though there will be relief knowing that their husband and father is released from suffering and into the presence of Christ. Who would be so cruel as to speak of joy under those circumstances? (Don James died at home on October 25, 2013. His final request was to have all of his children and grandchildren join him and Carol to sing familiar hymns together, speak of their faith, and receive communion from their pastor. For his text, the pastor choose John 11:25, "I am the resurrection and the life. He who believes in me will live, even though he dies, and whoever lives and believes in me will never die." Within hours, Don died at peace. The following week more than a thousand people gathered at the Hec Edmunson Basketball Arena on the University of Washington campus to celebrate Don's life. Whatever their faith position, every person who attended the service heard Jill, Don and Carol's daughter, sound the note of joy as she spoke on John 11:25.)

Jesus knew that his disciples would go through the throes of pain and grief because of his death. He did not dodge the issue, but said, "I tell you the truth, you will weep and mourn while the world rejoices. You will grieve, but your grief will turn to joy. A woman giving birth to a child has pain because her time has come, but when her baby is born she forgets the anguish because of her joy that a child is born into the world. So with you: Now is your time of grief, but I will see you again and you will rejoice, and no one will take away your joy" (John 16:20–22).

Critics may see in these words a Pollyanna approach to weeping, mourning, and grief. When we are going to through these experiences, especially death, it is an act of cruelty to say, "Don't cry, your grief will turn to joy." As a hospital chaplain, I learned the lesson of ministering to grieving people. Words of comfort and promises of Scripture have to give way to being present and listening. This pastoral principle came out of a follow-up study of the victims of the infamous Coconut Grove nightclub fire that claimed 492 lives. Circumstances divided the victims into two groups for counseling and therapy. The approach of one counseling group was to comfort the victims with words and help them forget the tragedy. The other group went through a totally different approach in which the persons were encouraged to talk candidly, weep openly, ask "Why?" and get angry if needed. In the time that followed, the first group took much longer to work through their grief and find healing than the second group. Presence and listening proved to be far more effective than words of comfort and promises of recovery.

Jesus allows time for his disciples to weep, mourn, and grieve after his death, but it is the promise of his presence that is the hope for their healing. Like the pain of childbirth, it is forgotten in the face of the baby who is born. This, of course, is the long-term view, because "Now we see but a poor reflection as in a mirror; then we will see face to face" (1 Cor 13:12). At that time, we will know the full measure of joy that no one can take away. But, even now, we are assured of the presence of the Holy Spirit in the pain of suffering.

Critics are baffled by the joy of believers who are suffering the most agonizing pain. At the 1989 World Congress on Evangelism held in Manila, the most memorable moment of all the sessions came when a Chinese man told his story of being arrested for his faith and condemned to work in an underground sewer with waste up to his knees. Yet, in that moment, he sang,

> I come to the garden alone, while the dew is still on the roses,
> And He walks with me and He talks with me, and He tells me I am his
> own; and the joy we share as we tarry there, none other has ever known.[1]

In his song, we learn the meaning of forgotten pain: "Now is your time of grief, but I will see you again and you will rejoice, and no one will take away your joy" (John 16:22).

The Joy of Disciplined Love

The love of Christ is not without an element of paradox. At the same time that it is unlimited and unconditional, to remain in his love and experience his joy we will obey his commands and discipline our desires. Jesus sets forth the principle: "As the Father has loved me, so have I loved you. Now remain in my love. If you obey my commands you will remain in my love, just as I have obeyed my Father's commands and remain in his love. I have told you this so that my joy may be in you and your joy may be complete" (John 15:9–11). In my later years I have taken on the practice of making my first words upon awakening, "This day I die—to self and sin—that I might

---

1. "In the Garden."

come alive with the mind and spirit of Jesus Christ." The discipline of these words draws my attention to areas of my life where I am weak and where I need to vow again to obey the commands of Christ. At the end of the day when I remember highlights and lowlights, wins and losses, there is almost always a joyous moment that goes on record in my daily journal. I know that this sounds a bit like a day in the life of a drunk who is a member of Alcoholics Anonymous, but perhaps we are more like one than we want to admit. Frank Gaberlein once told me about his son complaining, "Dad, you don't trust me." Frank answered, "Son, I don't trust myself." Honesty may bring us to the same confession. The joy of disciplined love is ours when we obey God's commands.

The Joy of Unlimited Asking

Almost every day I ask God to forgive for me—always asking and seldom quieting myself in his presence so that I can hear him speak. Jesus understands our asking. When his disciples were with him, they were completely dependent upon Jesus. If they had a question, he answered it; if they had a need, he met it. After he ascends to his Father, however, the disciples will have to go it alone. How will they cope? On what resources will they draw? Their personal resources will be still be severely limited, but Jesus gives them the promise, "In that day you will no longer ask me anything. I tell you the truth, my Father will give you whatever you ask in my name. Until now you have not asked for anything in my name. Ask and you will receive, and your joy will be complete" (John 16:23–24).

The promise is not a blank check for all our wants and wishes. We are to ask in the name of Jesus Christ. Immediately, some requests fall out of range. If our prayer of asking is selfish, devoid of love, or harmful to the common good, it will not be answered. But when spoken in his name for the fulfillment of his redemptive purpose, the promise is ours. Hudson Taylor, pioneer of nineteenth-century missions in China, proceeded with this confidence: "Depend upon it. God's work done in God's way will never lack God's supplies."[2] Even contemporary readers can feel the freedom and sense the joy in Taylor's words. Fund-raising is a burden that many Christian leaders carry today. Faith gets minimized by marketing techniques and campaign tactics. The gain may come in dollars, but at the expense of joy.

---

2. Taylor, *Hudson Taylor's Spiritual Secret*, 86.

Jesus' promise also has a personal application. In a consumer-driven culture based upon happiness, we can easily become victims of asking for our wants and wishes rather than our needs. I always remember my first reading of Henry David Thoreau as a junior high school student, and his statement, "He chooses to be rich by making his wants few, and supplying them himself."[3] A simple formula was devised with this passage in mind. When our wants are reduced to our needs, we are rich. Isn't that the same promise that Jesus gave his disciples? If we reduce our wants to our needs, we find full contentment and complete joy. Jesus' words make so much sense for Christians in a consumer-driven culture based upon happiness: "So do not worry, saying 'What shall we eat?' or 'What shall we drink?' or 'What shall we wear?' For the pagans run after all these things, and your heavenly Father knows that you need them. But seek first his kingdom and his righteousness, and all these things will be given to you as well" (Matt 6:31–33). When wants are reduced and needs are met, our joy will be complete.

Peter puts these thoughts together when he addresses the next generation of believers who did not have the privilege of seeing and knowing Jesus personally. It is Peter's promise of succession: "Though you have not seen him, you love him; and even though you do not see him now, you believe in him and are filled with an inexpressible and glorious joy, for you are receiving the goal of your faith, the salvation of your souls" (1 Pet 1:8–9). As with Peter, so with us: the promise of joy is a priceless leadership gift to those who succeed us.

The Oil of Joy

In my book *Power to Follow; Grace to Lead*, I devote three chapters to the primary tasks of leadership: (1) Seeing the vision; (2) Stating the mission; and (3) Setting the tone.[4] Leadership literature gives special emphasis to seeing the vision and stating the mission. Less is written about setting the tone, but as we review the teaching and experiences in the life of Jesus we realize that joy is the grace note in the music of his ministry. The writer of Hebrews felt the resonance of this accent when he introduced Jesus as the Son of God:

3. Emerson, "Thoreau."
4. McKenna, *Power to Follow*, 109–20.

You have loved righteousness and hated wickedness;
therefore God, your God, has set you above your companions
by anointing you with the oil of joy (Heb 1:9).

The writer is describing the *practical joy* that Jesus knew by serving in the name of his Father. Practical joy is then sustained by the *pure joy* of being in the presence of the Father, now as in worship and then as in heaven. Together, practical joy and pure joy blend into the grace note of *incarnate joy* that is intrinsic in value, independent of circumstances—even sacrifice and suffering—and given by the Holy Spirit as an anointing with oil.

Anointing with the oil of joy is a gift, not a goal, for Christian leadership. It is also difficult to define, but it is not difficult to detect. As a Christian leader, I adopted a system of "Four Firsts" for tone-setting: (a) the first door you enter; (b) the first person you meet; (c) the first speech you give; and (d) the first decision you make. Think about the first door you enter for a Christian organization. After hearing a nationally known architect for campus planning say that the entrance to a building sets the tone for the whole organization, I decided that I would pay special attention to the front doors of the campus. They can either give a warm welcome to those who enter or say "blah" in the gray word of functionality. If the entrance to our buildings do not say "welcome" and show humanized space, we are missing the first opportunity for tone-setting.

After entering a building, the first person you meet is a receptionist. If he or she greets you with a bright smile and a warm welcome, you transmit those words and spirit to the whole organization. Christian organizations with the spirit of joy cannot be faked. Because the oil of joy is contagious and pervasive, you can feel it from the moment you call the office or enter the door of a Christian organization. Richard Gross, president emeritus of Gordon College, taught me the meaning of "counter people." He was referring to the receptionist who answered the phone or greeted you upon arrival at the office. Dr. Gross said that he worked on the simple principle: "The tone that is set by the first person you meet sets the tone for the whole organization." He went on to say that once that tone is set, it is very difficult to change. The CEO, in particular, will be working against odds to change the tone that is set by the "counter person." I took the lesson seriously and asked to interview personally every candidate for the position of receptionist at the front desk in the administration building. It takes only a few questions to determine whether or not that person is the one whom you want to be a tone-setter for your organization.

The third "first" is the first speech that a leader gives. Rather than trying to see a new vision or state a revised mission, the first speech should be
a tone-setter for the leader. This means walking a fine line between realism
and optimism. The tendency in a first speech is to strike a glowing note
of unbridled optimism. Reality, however, says that every Christian organization has external and internal challenges that cannot be swept under
the rug. Also, as we have seen, anointing with the oil of joy recognizes the
paradox between success and suffering. So, instead of erring toward one
extreme or the other, the first speech of a new Christian leader should set
the tone of realistic optimism. The Apostle Paul strikes that note when he
writes, "where sin increased, grace increased all the more" (Rom 5:12).
John Wesley led with the same mantra. In his preaching he spoke realistically about human sin but more optimistically about God's grace. Consistent with the anointing of the oil of joy, the reality of sin is trumped by the
reality of grace.

Once the leader sets the tone with these three "firsts," the note of joy
is reinforced by the answers to these questions: (1) Do our people at every level of the organization find practical joy in the daily task of serving?
(2) Do our people sense the pure joy of God's presence when we come together in worship? and (3) Do our people know the incarnate joy of Christ
when we struggle with the paradox of suffering? As always, it is the Christian leader who answers these questions first with daily evidence of the oil
of joy in what is said or done and how it is expressed.

When the time comes for transition, then, a leader leaves his or her
successor a tone that tends to persist from generation to generation. Experience tells us why. Leaders tend to see the vision and state the mission of
an organization through the perspective of individual style and social circumstances. The tone of an organization is much more difficult to change.
Like the persistence of character in human personality and culture in social
organizations, tone tends to be contagious. If the tone set by a leader is a
note of joy, it will pervade the ranks and be infectious. If the tone is less
than joy, whether sullen or skeptical, it too will cross the ranks and infect
the generations. One of the most welcome gifts that a Christian leader can
leave to a successor is the affirmation of joy—unconditional in circum-
stance, practical in service, pure in worship, and incarnational in suffering.

9

The Gift of Anointing

"Sanctify them by the word of truth; your word is truth.
As you sent me into the world, I have sent them into the world.
For them I sanctify myself, that they too may be truly sanctified."

(JOHN 17:17–19)

IN ANTICIPATION OF SUCCESSION in leadership, Jesus has three specific prayers for his disciples whom he sends into a hostile world without his physical presence. As we have already seen, he first prays that the Holy Father will protect them from the evil one (chapter 7). Then we have felt him speak his desire that they will have the full measure of his joy within them (chapter 8). Now, we come to his third plea, that they may be sanctified through the word of truth. His first prayer invokes the power of the Father; his second prayer requests the joy of the Son; and his third prayer appeals to the anointing of the Spirit. Christian leaders are not intended to cower behind fortress walls in a hostile world. Assured of the protection of the Father and affirmed by the joy of Christ, we are expected to be on the offensive against evil under the anointing of the Holy Spirit.

A Holy Priesthood

Jesus' prayer for the sanctification of his disciples brings to mind the image of Moses preparing Aaron and his sons as priests who will make sacrifices for the sins of the people (Lev 8). An elaborate process of purifying begins with the washing of water (Lev 8:6), putting on sacred garments (Lev 8:8), and anointing their heads with oil (Lev 8:12–15). Aaron and his sons were then set apart to slaughter a bull for the blood sacrifice and a ram for the burnt offering (Lev 8:14–29). Then, with a mix of the oil of anointing and the blood of sacrifice, Moses sprinkled them and their garments to consecrate them to make the sacrifices for the sins of the people (Lev 9).

The sanctification of Aaron and his sons as priests goes through three steps: (1) Qualification by cleansing; (2) Ordination by separating; and (3) Service by anointing. When Jesus prays for the sanctification of his disciples he may well have these same steps in mind. To be qualified for office we need to be cleansed; to be ordained in office we need to be set apart; and to serve in office we need to be anointed.

The Sanctifying Word

A significant difference in the source of sanctification leaps out at us as we read the prayer of Jesus. The instrument for cleansing, separating, and anointing is not the command of Moses but the discipline of the word of truth. When Jesus prays, "Sanctify them by your word; your word is truth" (John 17:17), he brings us back to the fact that we cannot sanctify ourselves. The cleansing that us makes us holy comes when we submit ourselves to the discipline of the living and active word of God: "Sharper than any doubled-edged sword, it penetrates even to dividing soul and spirit, joints and marrow; it judges the thoughts and attitudes of the heart" (Heb 4:12). No cleansing is more penetrating or more complete. The writer of Hebrews goes on to say, "Nothing in all creation is hidden from God's sight. Everything is uncovered and laid bare before the eyes of him to whom we must give account" (Heb 4:13). Frightening? To be sure, but like the surgeon's clean, incisive cut, it is necessary for our healing. Peter, who knew so well what it meant to stand under the scrutiny of the Word, later wrote to God's elect across the earth, "Now that you have purified yourselves by obeying the truth so that you have sincere love for your brothers, love one another deeply, from the heart. For you have been born again, not of perishable seed, but of imperishable, through the living and enduring word of God" (1 Pet 1:22–23). His words remind us that we cannot sanctify ourselves—that is the work of the Holy Spirit. But we can purify our attitudes and actions by the cleansing power of the word of truth. Sanctification is both an act and a process. Before Jesus prayed for the sanctification of his disciples in the Prayer of Succession, he had said, "You are already clean because of the word I have spoken to you" (John 15:3). Now, he is saying that growing in holiness is also a process based upon periodic moments of self-examination according to the word of God. This same truth applies to the church of Jesus Christ as well as to his disciples. Paul admonishes husbands to love their wives "just as Christ loved the church and gave himself up for her to make her holy, cleansing her by the washing with water through the word, and to present her to himself as a radiant church, without stain or wrinkle or any other blemish, but holy and blameless" (Eph 5:25–27). A tall order, indeed, but not an impossibility, either for us or for the church.

A Consecrated Leader

If Christian leadership can be narrowed down to one differentiating principle, it is found in the words of Jesus, "For them I sanctify myself, that they too may be truly sanctified" (John 17:19). Even though Jesus is without sin he submits himself to the scrutiny of the word of God for the sake of his disciples. He is not speaking hypothetically. Within hours after this commitment is made he will be in the garden of Gethsemane in a life-and-death struggle between his will to live and God's call to die. Sweat like drops of blood shows the same intensity that we know when the word of God convicts and calls us to total sacrifice. Jesus does not sanctify himself just for the sake of his disciples, but for himself as well.

Consecration or "being set apart for a holy task" follows cleansing in the process of sanctification. Jesus, in his garden prayer, has to make the final decision about his destiny. Will he be set apart in order to die for the sins of the world? Or is there another way? We know the answer as he pleads for his life with the Father time and time again. Finally, in one last appeal the die are cast: "Abba, Father, everything is possible for you. Take this cup from me. Yet not what I will, but what you will" (Mark 14:36). His consecration is complete. Cleansed and made holy, consecrated and set apart, he leads his disciples by the way of the cross.

The Anointing Spirit

In the wilderness Jesus goes through the cleansing process that makes him holy. In the garden he comes to the moment of consecration when he is set apart to die on the cross as the only way for our sins to be forgiven. Between these experiences there are other episodes and events that reinforce his cleansing and reaffirm his consecration. His sanctification is not complete, however, without the anointing of the Spirit of God. At least twice in the Gospel record we read of God the Father claiming Jesus Christ as his Son, whom he loved, and with whom he was pleased (Matt 3:17 and Matt 17:5). In the gentle dove or bright cloud that descended in those moments, Jesus is anointed and his sanctification is complete. The disciples, however, will have to wait until Jesus has ascended into heaven and the tongues of fire at Pentecost cleanse, consecrate, and anoint them by the power of the Holy Spirit.

The Oil of Anointing

Sanctification is a doctrine of biblical faith that has many faces. Whether the gift of the Spirit at the time of justification or a second work of grace, whether instantaneous event or gradual experience, whether accepted as a common gift or attested to by a special gift, one thing is sure: it is an experience of cleansing, consecration, and anointing that is exemplified by Jesus Christ as his gift of succession to his disciples and to all believers. Yet, when we think about the legacy of leadership, the example of sanctification is seldom mentioned. In fact, after reading scores of profiles for recruiting leaders for Christian organizations, I do not recall one instance where sanctification was noted as a qualifier for the position. The expectation deserves another look.

It doesn't take a biblical scholar to know an anointed Christian leader. The example of sanctification sets the spiritual pace for all followers. The leader is made holy by the cleansing of the Word, set apart by consecration in Christ, and empowered to serve sacrificially by the anointing of the Holy Spirit. Thank God, he has given me the opportunity to see and know so many sanctified people who set the pace for all of us:

- James Gregory, my first theology professor, who likened sanctification to any thread in the fabric of life having the text, tone, and color of the whole cloth;

- J. C. McPheeters, my seminary president, who preached holiness with vigor and lived it with a twinkle in his eye;

- Paul Rees, my seminary trustee, who wrote notes to me every week with gems of warning and wisdom;

- James Earl Massey, my preaching model, whose gift for music was played on the piano and in the pulpit;

- Lloyd John Oglivie, my pastoral model, who proved that you can be holy in Hollywood;

- Rebecca Manley Pippert, my colleague in Christ, who urged us to get the salt out of the shaker;

- Mark Hatfield, my political hero, who taught me that the "quiet sovereignty" of the Lord is still the best for us;

- Robert Fine, my university pastor, who taught me the tone of "Great Todays; Better Tomorrows";

- Elizabeth Elliot, my loving critic, who tolerated "no monkey business" in kingdom matters;

- Kenneth Hansen, my executive mentor, who warned me against the dangers of being articulate;

- Fred Smith Sr., my wisest friend, who taught me to watch the feet of preachers to see if they are dancing;

- Shirley Ort, my adopted daughter, who taught me that good governance is more poetry than prose;

- Martin Marty, my scholar of scholars, who taught me to listen when wisdom speaks.

What do these leaders have in common? It is the development of character through the discipline of the Word. They have taken seriously Paul's admonition to the members of the Philippian church, "Finally, brothers [and sisters], whatever is true, whatever is noble, whatever is right, whatever is pure, whatever is lovely, whatever is admirable—if anything is excellent or praiseworthy—think about such things" (Phil 4:8). With modesty, then, the apostle adds, "Whatever you have learned or received or heard from me, or seen in me—put it into practice" (Phil 4:9). What a priceless gift of leadership. It is daring his readers to frisk his life for any evidence of the false, ignoble, wrong, impure, ugly, or despicable. This is the platinum standard of holiness to which we are called. This is Christ-centered leadership at its highest and best. Cleansing by the Word is both the starting point and the continuing discipline for our sanctification.

But, we no sooner make the claim for cleansing than we are brought to a screeching halt. Like a turtle on a fence post, we did not get there by our own doing. Only through Christ's consecration to be set apart and die for our sins are we made holy. We can have the motive but only he has the means. Our sanctification moves from cleansing to consecration when he sets us apart for a holy task and seals our calling with his ordination. Like Jesus in the garden, it may be a struggle of wills. But when the final word is said, it must be, "Yet, not what I will, but what you will" (Mark 14:36).

Once we are qualified to lead by the cleansing of the Word and commissioned to lead by the consecration of Christ, the finishing touch will be the oil of anointing administered by the Holy Spirit. The beauty and grace of the Holy Spirit in the life of the Christian leader cannot be faked. P. T. Barnum had it right when he said, "You can fool some of the people some of the time, but you cannot fool all of the people all of the time." These words were spoken by the master of false faces and the magician of sensory illusion. Jesus, on the other hand, had a nose for the genuine. Pretenders to spiritual anointing were invariably unmasked in his presence. The seven woes pronounced upon the teachers of the law and the Pharisees who pretended to be holy begin with the indictment, "You hypocrites!" (Matt 23:13–32). The apostles, too, had the gift for perceiving deception. When Simon the Sorcerer, who did wonders of magic before his conversion, tried to buy the gift of the Holy Spirit, Peter scorched him: "To hell with you and your money! How dare you think that you could buy the gift of God? You have no share or place in this ministry for your heart is not honest before God. All you can do now is to repent of this wickedness of yours and pray earnestly to God that the evil intention of your heart may be forgiven. For I can see inside of you, and I see a man bitter with jealousy and bound with his own sin" (Acts 8:20–21, *Phillips Modern Translation*). Sooner or later, every pretender to the anointing of the Holy Spirit will be exposed by perceptive people who have the mind of Christ. Likewise, every Christian leader who has the anointing of the Spirit will have a lasting legacy that is passed on from generation to generation.

When all of these thoughts come into focus, we who lead will have the gift of anointing as an example for our successors. The gift will include the practice of periodic submission to the cleansing truth of the Word of God and evidence of growth in holiness. We can also present them with the evidence that we are qualified by purity of character and commissioned with the gifts of grace. Finally, as the sign and seal of our cleansing and our consecration, we will have the gracious anointing of the Spirit so that in the transition of leadership we will be able to say, "Whatever you have learned or received or heard from me, or seen in me—put it into practice" (Phil 4:9).

PART III

The Legacy of Love

10

The Gift of Anticipation

"My prayer is not for them alone.
I pray also for those who will believe
in me through their message."

(JOHN 17:20–21)

AFTER JESUS REPORTS THAT he has been true to his trust of doing the Father's will and true to his task of developing mature disciples who are now ready to lead, he lifts his eyes to see a future that is soon to be. His vision is not disconnected from reality. Beginning with his nearby disciples, he foresees them and their followers forming an unbroken line of succession stretching through generation after generation until the Father's eternal purpose of human salvation comes to full fruition.

If there is one word that defines the quality of great leadership, it is "anticipation." In the book *Maestro*, by Roger Nierenberg, the conductor of a symphony orchestra teaches us that a leader lives in three time zones. Applied to music, there is the time zone of the past in the written score, the time zone of the present in the conductor's baton, and the time zone of the future in the unified sound of great music in the conductor's mind. All three time zones come together in the movement of the conductor's baton as the orchestra soars beyond the notes to the awe-inspiring realm of musical artistry.[1]

1. Nierenberg, *Maestro*, 86.

Jesus is the maestro. Grounded in the time zone of the Word, he anticipates the time zone of the coming kingdom through the deft and delicate touch of his Spirit in the time zone of his earthly ministry. No wonder his disciples never lost the sense of holy awe that took them across the earth and through the fire. To be leaders worthy of his name, we too must live in three time zones, faithfully honoring the Word, deftly directing our disciples by the Holy Spirit, and always anticipating the glorious promise of the kingdom of God on earth.

Christians should always be criticized as leaders who are "ahead of their time." If, like Jesus, we sight along the line of succession, we will see beyond our time and tenure to an era when the ministry we lead will have influence and impact foreseen only in our imaginations. We are not talking about a figment of the imagination as splashed on the screen of the latest video game. Steve Jobs is the poster child for "insanely great" ideas coming out of a creative mind and proving to be immensely successful.[2] His flight of ideas, however, was not disconnected from sound thinking about integrated or "i" systems that produced iPhones, iPads, iPods, and iTunes. Philosophers acclaim "reasoned imagination" as the highest virtue, meaning creative vision that springs from grounding in solid facts. Jesus shows us the way with the reasoned proof of the Father's authority and his disciples' maturity. On this evidence, Jesus can stretch his imagination to its full potential. Psychologists raise this virtue another notch to "moral imagination," defined as the "humility to see the world as it is and the audacity to see it as it could be."[3] The secular mind-set prizes audacity to see the world as it could be, but not necessarily the humility to see the world as it is. Utopian fantasies, such as Plato's *Republic*, Thomas More's *Utopia*, and B. F. Skinner's *Walden Two* are evidence of audacity minus humility. Jesus, however, is not indulging in fantasy when he anticipates his disciples going "into all the world" through the line of succession (Mark 16:15). Earlier in his prayer, he spares no words when he describes the bitter hostility of the world and the vicious attacks of Satan that his disciples will encounter. Yet, as we have already seen, against that opposition his disciples will be true to the Word, sure in their identity, filled with joy, and holy in character. Reason, humility, and audacity all come together when Jesus imagines the future of the faith through the line of succession.

2. Isaacson, *Steve Jobs*, 111.
3. "Leadership Model."

There is more. As you feel your way into the heart of Jesus when he prays for generations of disciples yet unborn, you sense the legacy of love at work in his passion for the Father's purpose and his embrace of those who will follow him. Imagination grounded in reason, tempered by humility, inspired by audacity, and fired by passion is the gift of anticipation that Jesus leaves his successors, including us.

At the very onset of his ministry, Jesus encounters Nathanael sitting under a fig tree. Nathanael is awed by Jesus' foresight into his character as an Israelite without blame. Out of that awe, faith takes hold, and Nathanael confesses, "Rabbi, You are the Son of God. You are the King of Israel." Jesus humbly accepts his accolade but quickly adds, "You will see greater things than that. I tell you that you shall see heaven open and the angels of God ascending and descending upon the Son of Man" (John 1:43–51). In the lessons of this encounter, we get an advance glimpse into the gift of anticipation.

Risking Our Faith

To receive the gift of anticipation, we need to *risk our faith*. Nathanael was a man of faith who lived so close to God that Jesus gave him his highest commendation as an Israelite in whom there was no deceit, or as some scholars suggest, "there was no Jacob in him." Jacob, of course, held the reputation as the epitome of deceit until he wrestled with God. Nathanael is just the opposite—the model of integrity meditating under a fig tree and waiting for the coming of the Messiah. At the same time, he nursed a bias against Nazareth, the despised town in Galilee reputed to produce nothing good. When Philip arrives and gives him the personal invitation to come and see Jesus of Nazareth, the flaw in Nathanael's thinking is exposed. "Can anything good come out of Nazareth?" is a sarcastic question based upon an elitist bias. Rather than arguing the point with him, Philip invites him to "Come and see." He dares to counter Nathanael's skepticism with the empirical test. His risk is worth it. One glimpse of the Master and Nathanael bows to confess, "Rabbi. You are the Son of God, you are the King of Israel."

In his book *Future Edge,* Joel Barker popularized the term and concept "paradigm shift."[4] A paradigm is the framework through which we see the world. A Christian, for instance, is a person who sees the world through the framework of biblical revelation, with its central focus upon the incarnation

4. Barker, *Future Edge*, 3.

of the Lord Jesus Christ. How, then, does a Christian respond to revolutionary changes in society, such as the current paradigm shift into the cyber age of high technology? One option is to hunker down behind a barricade around our faith in the posture of what Barker calls "paradigm paralysis."[5] The other option is to risk our faith in a world of change without sacrificing one iota of our convictions about biblical revelation or the primacy of Jesus Christ.

Barker illustrates "paradigm paralysis" with a humorous story. A man is driving on a treacherous mountain road. As he comes around a hairpin curve he sees a red convertible, driven by a blonde woman, careening wildly back and forth across the road in front of him. He slams on the brakes and heads for the shoulder to avoid a collision. At the last second, the oncoming car swerves to miss him and as it skids by the woman driver screams, "Pig!" Enraged, he yells back, "Wench!" In his anger he steps on the gas, hits the curve at full speed, and crashes into the biggest pig he has ever seen standing in the middle of the road. He is a victim of "paradigm paralysis" with all of his fixed assumptions about a careening red convertible driven by a blonde yelling, "Pig!"

Nathanael might also have been the victim of "paradigm paralysis" in his bias against Nazareth. All he had to do was tell Philip, "I don't do Nazareth," and the gift of anticipation would have been lost.

Leonard Sweet, a popular author and fellow educator, keynoted a Leadership Network Conference devoted to the theme "The Church in the Twenty-First Century." After citing changes and challenges that the church will face in the years ahead, he called his listeners to take the risk of faith by reciting this litany:

> The world is a better place because Michelangelo didn't say, "I don't do ceilings";
>
> The world is a better place because Martin Luther didn't say, "I don't do doors";
>
> The world is a better place because John Wesley didn't say, "I don't do fields";
>
> The world is a better place because Moses didn't say, "I don't do rivers";
>
> The world is a better place because Noah didn't say, "I don't do arks";
>
> The world is a better place because Jeremiah didn't say, "I don't do weeping";
>
> The world is a better place because Amos didn't say, "I don't do speeches";

5. Ibid., 155–56.

The world is a better place because Rahab didn't say, "I don't do carpets";

The world is a better place because Ruth didn't say, "I don't do mothers-in-law";

The world is a better place because David didn't say, "I don't do giants";

The world is a better place because Peter didn't say, "I don't do Gentiles";

The world is a better place because Mary didn't say, "I don't do virgin births";

The world is a better place because Mary Magdalene didn't say, "I don't do feet";

The world is a better place because John didn't say, "I don't do deserts";

The world is a better place because Paul didn't say, "I don't do letters";

The world is a better place because Jesus didn't say, "I don't do crosses."[6]

When we answer Jesus' call, "Follow me," we will drop the "I don't do" mentality and always be moving forward at a risk. He took the chance of leaving popular acclaim to go into the next village, facing mortal threat by setting his face toward Jerusalem, and telling his disciples "Let's roll" on his way to the cross. The risk of faith goes with the gift of anticipation.

Seeing Beyond Ourselves

It is easy to talk about ourselves, our time, and our achievements. Jesus despoils that narcissistic impulse when he asks us to see beyond ourselves. Although Nathanael is a man of faith, Jesus says to him, "You believe because I told you that I saw you under a fig tree. You will see greater things than that" (John 1:50). When paradigms are shifting in changing times, only those who see the promise of greater things will survive. When Joel Barker envisions the future, he says that only those who excel will survive and only those who innovate will compete. Barker names these people "paradigm pioneers."[7]

I am amazed at the creative impulses of secular leaders who are grappling with the vision of greater things as we shift to the paradigm of greater things. When we were developing a "smart campus" at Asbury Theological Seminary in the 1990s I had a day of coaching on high-tech teaching at Ball State University. In one session I had a robot camera called Panavision under my control as I moved about the room, pushing buttons on the

6. Sweet, "The Church in the 21st Century." Used with permission.

7. Barker, *Future Edge*, 71–83.

monitor attached to my belt, and zooming the camera in on the blackboard for teaching emphasis. Later, I had dinner with three of the presidents of high-tech corporations who were equipping our studios and laboratories at the seminary. When I told them about the 220 delegates who would be coming to the campus for the North American section of the World Methodist Council, they asked, "How can we demonstrate the potential of high technology for the ministry of the church?" My mind began to spin a dream that I thought would stump them. I said, "I would like to see Asbury Seminary connected by two-way interactive television with Dr. Donald English, international president of the World Methodist Council, in London." They put their heads together and I overheard such words as "uplink," "downlink," and "London studio." Then, their heads popped up and they said, "We can do it with the technology that we already have. The biggest problem will be coordinating Dr. English's schedule with the American time zone." In their response, I saw that corporations are in the lead, adjusting to a global economy, re-engineering their organizations to cope with new information, developing partnerships with former competitors, and envisioning new markets even in debtor nations.

With regret, I fear that we who are leaders of the church are going in the opposite direction. Martin Marty notes that the religious world has turned inward at the same time that the secular world is opening up.[8] Rather than following the lead of Jesus to see beyond ourselves, we are victims of paradigm paralysis. Marty writes:

- we are preoccupied with *individual religious experience* at the expense of *communal meaning*;

- we have turned our attention to *private faith* at the expense of *public responsibility*;

- we have emphasized *personal meaning* in religion over the strength of *belonging*;

- we are absorbed by *local and provincial* religious issues at the expense of *global and ecumenical* concerns, and;

- we are attuned to *affective impulses* at the expense of *intellectual inquiry*.

8. Professor Marty and the author searched the volumes of his writing for the source of this quote without success. Finally, in his inimitable way, Marty suggested I say, "Here I am quoting a guy named Marty who, somewhere or other, may or may not have written that." Used with permission.

If Marty's analysis is accurate, it appears as if the secular world has its head in a cloud while the religious world is still in a fog.

Yet, the rich history of Christian faith gives us a heritage of persons who see beyond themselves to the vision of greater things. In our Wesleyan tradition, for instance, John Wesley broke the traditional paradigm for preaching when he left the high pulpit of the Anglican Church to stand on a small rise in the open fields to offer millers and miners the gospel of Jesus Christ. Francis Asbury broke the traditional paradigm of evangelism when he left the established church of the Eastern Seaboard and struck out on horseback over the Allegheny and Appalachian Mountains to open the western frontier. In succession with such paradigm pioneers, we receive the gift of anticipation and see beyond ourselves.

Expecting the Unexpected

With the gift of anticipation, we will also come to *expect the unexpected.*

Jesus bursts the boundaries of the expected when he promises Nathanael, "You shall see the heavens open, and the angels of God ascending and descending upon the Son of Man" (John 1:51). With these words, Jesus shows us that he is a "paradigm buster." Nathanael will join Jacob in the rare experience of seeing the heavens open and the transcendent God touch down on earth in human experience.

Jesus' response reminds us again that God is full of surprises. Nathanael bows before Jesus and confesses that he is the "Son of God" and "King of Israel." As true as these words are, they are still within the limits of the Old Testament paradigm for the coming Messiah. To acknowledge him as the "Son of God" is to confess his heavenly authority; to acclaim him as "King of Israel" is to express his earthly authority. Both confessions are true, but incomplete. With the highest compliment, Jesus invites Nathanael into the company of Jacob, who has a dream in which he sees angels ascending and descending on a ladder with the Lord God standing at the top (Gen 28:12–13). Heaven touches earth again in this image, but not in the kingship of an earthly empire. The Son of Man comes from questionable birth, a despised village, and a humble vocation. All that Nathanael expects has to give way to the unexpected. His Messiah will not be the conquering king; he will be the humble servant. Power will give way to love and the salvation of Israel will be expanded to include the whole world. When the unexpected is seen through the eyes of love, there are no limits. The sweep of the unexpected includes an endless line of succession until Christ comes again, with unlimited grace for all people of all nations, and a universal church embracing all believers.

Jesus is asking Nathanael to join the ranks of crazy dreamers. Eddie Fox, evangelist for the World Methodist Council, tells of visiting Germany after the Berlin Wall fell. He asked Christian leaders, "Did you expect the wall to fall in your lifetime?" They answered, "No." He asked again, "Did anyone expect the wall to fall in your lifetime?" "Well, yes," they answered. "There were some crazy dreamers who thought that it might be possible." Eddie said, "Take me to meet your crazy dreamers."

Peter Kuzmic, Toms Distinguished Professor of World Missions and European Studies at Gordon-Conwell Theological Seminary, gives Eddie's story an insightful spin. When I asked him to explain what appeared to be impossible with the fall of the Berlin Wall, Peter simply said, "Never put a period where God puts a comma." Crazy dreamers are comma people. Tony Campolo, another good friend and brother, raises the meaning of God's work for the impossible to its highest level. In his best-known book and sermon, he repeats time and time again, "It's Friday; Sunday's comin'!"[9] Resurrection hope is the perspective that fires the imagination and kindles the love for the unexpected. Just as Jesus promised Nathanael that he would see "greater things," we who are Christian leaders will see far beyond our own time and tenure. Of course, our farewell speeches will be grounded on "then" and built on "now," but we will never put a period at that point in time. To give our successors the gift of anticipation, we will speak of "not yet" as the word of hope, not in predetermining the tasks for our successors, but by putting a comma at the end of our career.

We have received the gift of anticipation from our predecessors. Now it is our turn. God wants us to pass on the legacy of love, risking our faith, seeing beyond ourselves, and expecting the unexpected. When we do, we will sight along the line of succession and see the gift of greater things for the one who follows us.

9. Campolo, *It's Friday, Sunday's Comin'*.

11

The Gift of Accord

"My prayer is not for them alone. I pray also
for those who believe in me through their message,
that all of them may be one, Father, just as you are in me
and I am in you. May they also be in us so that the world
may believe that you have sent me."

(JOHN 17:20–21)

VISIONARY LEADERS SEE FAR down the road. With the shadow of the cross looming over his head, we would not be surprised if Jesus ended his prayer by sanctifying himself so that his disciples would be sanctified. Instead, his head lifts and his vision clears as he sees future generations who will believe in him through the message of the apostles. His prayer is very simple. He asks only that they may know the oneness that he has with his Father so that the world will believe in him. These words stretch through the centuries and touch down in our time. Jesus is still praying that we might be one in our *relationship* with him, one in our *association* with each other, and one in our *witness* to the world. This is the long-term legacy of every Christian leader. Oneness in Christ is a gift of succession that Jesus leaves us.

The Oneness of Relationship

A favorite descriptor for our evangelical faith is to say that we have a "relationship" with Jesus Christ. The term is ambiguous. A similar idea is conveyed when young people speak of "being in a relationship." The meaning can range from serious dating to exclusive cohabiting. It does imply that their affections are reserved for a single person, but not with the lifelong commitment of marriage.

Jesus lifts the meaning of being in a "relationship" when he speaks about his oneness with his Father. As we have already seen, that relationship is defined by *trust* as the Father gives his Son total authority over all people for the purpose of giving them eternal life (John 17:2), by *truth* as Father and Son affirm their common identity (17:3), and by *task* as they glorify each through the completed work of Jesus Christ (17:4–5).

Our "relationship" with Jesus Christ must be defined by these same criteria. Can he trust us as we trust him? Are we identified with him as he is identified with us? Is he glorified in us as we are glorified in him? Suddenly, we find ourselves plunging from a shallow relationship as buddies to familial depth as brothers or sisters for whom blood is thicker than water. As an Irishman, I remember my grandfather saying, "We fight with each other, but don't let anyone attack us. We will die for each other." Opponents of Christianity need to keep this in mind. We may occasionally fight with each other as a family, but we will always die for each other in the faith.

Our relationship with Jesus Christ in trust, truth, and task becomes very practical in conflict. More than once, I found myself at loggerheads with faculty colleagues in Christian higher education over issues of governance that smacked of the old management-labor mentality. Our conversations were paralyzed until we went back to the baseline of our common relationship with Jesus Christ as our Savior and Lord. Once we agreed on that point, we could progress to the step of reaffirming our common commitment to the ministry of Christian higher education. We could then ask, "Can we trust each other as Christ trusts us?"; "Can we affirm our common identity in Christ?"; and "Can we honor each other's work for the sake of Jesus Christ?" Without an answer to these questions, conflicts in the Christian community can be more vicious than any dog-eat-dog battles in secular politics. In the words of the once-popular song, "You always hurt the one you love."

The Oneness of Association

Jesus leaves no doubt that he anticipates a community of believers based upon the confession of his name (Matt 16:18). He does not have in mind a monolithic structure that stands alone to represent his kingdom on earth. Rather, as he tells the woman at the well, he sees the time coming "when the true worshipers will worship the Father in spirit and truth, for they are the kind of worshiper the Father seeks" (John 4:23). It is with this oneness in spirit and truth that Jesus asks in his Prayer of Succession, "May they be brought to complete unity to let the world know that you sent me and have loved them even as you have loved me" (John 17:23). His prayer for "complete unity" does not begin with an institution based upon structure, but in an association based upon relationship. Specifically, the same oneness of relationship that his disciples have with Christ individually is now extended to the unity of their association together. Returning to the profile of characteristics for the body of Christ following Pentecost, the beauty of their association together stands out in the words, "They broke bread in their homes and ate together with glad and sincere hearts, praising God and enjoying the favor of all the people" (Acts 3:46). If we are looking for a test of vitality in the body of Christ, here it is: when we worship, we are together in reverence and awe; when we eat we are together in spontaneous gladness and joy.

One of the highest of compliments paid to Asbury Theological Seminary came when a visiting team for accreditation as a nationally-recognized graduate school of theology included this commendation in their final report: "We have never seen a place where people find so many reasons to get together and celebrate." The reference was not to the formal structure of the seminary but to the informal spirit of the association. Imagine applying this standard to the evaluation of our churches and organizations. To the statistics of growth we would add the decibels of gladness. This is not always the case. Some Christian congregations and organizations are like the missionary who said, "I love the people of Africa, but I do not like them." This should not be the case. You can tell when the fresh winds of Pentecost are blowing through a church or an organization. Members of the body of Christ not only love each other, they actually like each other.

The idea of the body of Christ as an association has many implications. I often recall the national conference in 1976 when 700 colleges and universities that claim to be under the broad umbrella of Christian higher education came together to think and plan for the future of the sector.

Extremes ran from liberal institutions that gave the Christian faith only a wink and a nod to fundamentalist institutions that laid claim to a special corner on the truth. In the opening session, these differences divided the house. Then, the chaplain of a renowned eastern university whose rich history in the faith had become a faint memory gave a devotion in preparation for a closing communion. Taking his text from 1 Corinthians 12:3, he deftly drew his listeners together with the truth, "no one can say, 'Jesus is Lord' except by the Holy Spirit." Theological, historical, and denominational differences seemed to melt away in that common confession, and when the invitation to the Lord's table was given, almost every delegate to the conference went forward to take communion. I knelt between the president of a Roman Catholic university and the president of a Pentecostal college. In that moment, by the Holy Spirit, we became associated as one in the confession of Jesus Christ as Lord.

As I think about other associations of believers with whom I have been affiliated, I realize how far I have come from my exclusive roots. In the holiness tabernacle where I grew up, the pastor railed against compromising Christians who joined ecumenical associations, even the local ministerial organization. In my career, however, I served as an officer in the National Association of Evangelicals, World Methodist Council, Bread for the World, and the Evangelical Environmental Network. Criticism could follow some of my choices, but in each case I had the opportunity to join with other believers in a specific cause and help keep a biblical balance in the effort. How far should we go in joining such causes? I recall Francis Schaeffer's pro-life campaign in which he invited "co-belligerents" or persons who would usually be considered adversaries of Christian faith to join him in opposing abortion. Jerry Falwell took a similar stance with the Moral Majority. Although Schaeffer and Falwell were Christian leaders, they welcomed into their ranks anyone who supported their social cause. Although common convictions on moral issues created these associations, they fell short on the oneness of the body of Christ whose members love and like each other because of their Spirit-prompted confession that Jesus Christ is Lord. We can be sure that new associations will germinate continuously in a changing culture where special needs bring believers together in common cause. Although we may find ourselves aligned with a diverse company of faith or nonfaith from time to time, we must not mistake these alliances for an association of believers whose confession of Christ precedes their commitment to a common cause. Whenever the fresh winds of Pentecost blow through our ranks, our staid and stodgy structures will be challenged. We must remember, however, that our informal associations are only temporary. As the Spirit of God continues to breathe on us, we will move on.

The Oneness of Witness

We know that Jesus is praying for the spiritual unity of all people who receive him and his message. The body of Christ cannot be confined within one human institution. At the same time, when Christ prays for oneness in our association together, he is referring to our corporate as well as our individual witness. The fire of the Holy Spirit would meld a ragtag team of apostles and disciples into the fellowship of believers so aptly described in Acts 2:42–47 as a unified force through whom "the Lord added to their number daily those who were being saved." From its beginnings at Jerusalem, then, the church of Jesus Christ was planted wherever the apostles and their disciples were dispersed by choice or by force. By natural process, the church of Jesus advanced from an informal association to a formal organization and on to a social institution. It is false to assume that an institutional church is inherently detrimental to a dynamic witness of the faith. To the contrary, primary social institutions are formed in order to serve a human need that cannot be met without an organized structure, a regularized process, and a plan for sharing resources. The first church of Jesus Christ in Jerusalem exactly fits this pattern. The apostles led the organization in teaching, fellowship, communion, and prayer. All members met daily in the temple courts and in their respective homes for worship, dining, and celebrations of praise. In witness of their oneness they pooled their resources to meet the needs of every member. Did the beginnings of a formal organization stifle their witness? Tonal words such as *awe, glad, sincere, praising,* and *enjoying* tell us "No." Jesus' prayer for the oneness of association as a witness to the world is answered when we read, "And the Lord added to their number daily those who were being saved" (Acts 2:47).

Sooner or later, associations that spring up spontaneously and grow exponentially in response to a common cause will run into the reality of limited resources and the need for division of labor in leadership. The body of Christ that was created by the tongues of fire and the rushing winds of Pentecost is a prime example. Acts 6:1–8 succinctly states the case for a conflict over resources with the underlying issues of ethnic differences and ancient jealousy over status and privilege. As we have already seen, the apostles solved the problem by using Spirit-guided wisdom to create a simple organization based upon a division of labor involving the election of seven deacons to wait on tables and make fair allotments of food to the contending factions. This action freed the twelve apostles so that they could give exclusive attention to prayer and the ministry of the word.

With this action of enlightened leadership, the body of Christ was now posed to become a dynamic social movement. The passionate call to be a movement again is being heard from every sphere of Christian faith today, whether in a world congress, a denominational conference, a megachurch federation, or a free-ranging para-church ministry. Instruments for this call come in the extremes, from a renewal of Pentecost to the lofty goals of a strategic plan. When reality checks in, however, we must remember that a social movement that transforms a culture comes at a very high price. In the case of the early New Testament church, the movement was launched by the martyrdom of Stephen the deacon. His death led to the diaspora, or dispersion, of believers to far-flung fields. Jewish leaders took the new movement so seriously that they commissioned Saul to hunt down and quash this faction that was growing exponentially in influence centers as prominent as Damascus, Syria.

An unforgettable memory comes to mind. In 1980 my wife and I hosted a choir tour to Asia for Seattle Pacific University. Manila, Tokyo, Taipei, Seoul, and Bangkok were all on the choir schedule. It is the concert at Young Nak Presbyterian Church in Seoul that can never be forgotten. On the day of the concert we were told that 750,000 South Korean soldiers had been baptized as their confession of faith. When we arrived at the church that evening we were astounded by the sight. Fifteen thousand worshipers had come for Wednesday night service. Although our University choir performed with polished and spirited excellence it was the sound of birdlike voices singing "How Great Thou Art" that I still hear.

After the service I asked the pastor, "How do you explain what is happening among your troops and among your people?" He did not hesitate, but said, "You must remember that we are only one generation from martyrdom. Almost every family has been touched." He was referring to the oppression of Japanese occupation until 1953, the massacre of Christians in the split with North Korea, and the continuing regime of Kim Il-Sung in the persecution of Christians and their churches. Yet, during this same period, the percentage of Christians grew from 4 percent in 1950 to 18 percent in 1980. Sam Moffett, a pioneer missionary to Korea, when asked how to explain this "leap" in the growth of the Korean church, surprised his inquirer by saying, "For years we have simply held up to these people the Word of God and the Holy Spirit has done the rest."[1] It is the work of the Holy Spirit, not persecution, that explains the movement of Christianity that has swept South Korea. Yet, as the Presbyterian pastor said, persecution is a factor.

In another example, Martin Luther King Jr. is credited with the beginning of the civil rights movement. The story, however, turns on the ugly moment in Birmingham, Alabama when Bull O'Connor sicced his attack dogs on the children who were marching on the mayor's office. King opposed the plan of his associate, James Bevel, to risk the lives of children at the front edge of protest. But when CBS TV captured the picture of a dog viciously attacking a child, Bevel led the cheers, triumphantly exclaiming, "We've got a movement! We've got a movement!"[2] The march was called off and Martin Luther King Jr. used the episode to advance his agenda of nonviolent protest. Civil rights became a movement when a child paid the price.

A word of caution to Christian leaders: when we call for the church to become a movement again, we must count the cost and be ready to pay the price.

In the case of the early New Testament church, we see the pattern: an association becomes a movement and a movement becomes an institution through the process of a maturing organization. When Paul founded churches at every stop along the way of his missionary journeys, he had to count on the development of an organization that would sustain the movement after he moved on. In response to this need, he showed the churches a dying world as the sole reason for their existence, added the charge to make Christ known, and backed it up with the authority given to him as an apostle of Jesus Christ. To implement this statement of mission, Paul gave the churches a model of organization based upon the unity of the human body with the diversity of its functioning parts and the unity of administration based upon its diversity of gifts and roles (chapter 4). Once these fundamental principles were in place, the early New Testament church had all it needed to become a primary institution unified in purpose and empowered to make a long-term impact on a secular culture and a pagan society.

1. Moffett, "What Makes the Korean Church Grow?"
2. M. Friedman, *Free at Last*.

At this point, we need to stop and deal with the criticism of what is called the "institutional church" today. Yes, I share the view of Reinhold Neibuhr, who compared the institutional church to Noah's ark by noting, "If it weren't for the storm outside, we couldn't stand the stench inside."[3] But something more is at stake. The loss of confidence in the institutional church has been diagnosed to death. Changes in the social environment, led by the loss of established authority, and failures in religious institutions, led by the shift from serving others to saving itself, highlight reasons for the loss of confidence. However true these reasons may be, our diagnosis needs to go deeper. Has the church put itself into the margins of moral influence by losing its calling to be a primary or mediating institution in the society where it exists? A mediating institution is defined as the cultural influence that conveys the norms and values of the society to individuals so as to integrate them into the community and the culture. More specifically, a mediating institution is also one that stands between the extremes of dictatorship in the sphere of the state and the chaos of anarchy in the sphere of the individual. While wringing our hands over the intrusion of government into our private lives, we may be sidestepping the fact that the church has forfeited its role as a mediating institution in favor of becoming culturally relevant, one generational, size sensitive, relief oriented, and missions minded. The case is made by the evidence of the flight of the white church to the suburbs and the decline of the black church in the ghetto. Just at the time when society desperately needs the mediating and sustaining influence of the church for its systemic maladies, the institution has been co-opted by the culture, embraced a popular cause, misinterpreted the meaning of counterculture, or fled the scene. Irony attends the efforts of the church to maintain the benefits of a mediating institution, such as tax and religious exemptions and clergy allowances, when the historical basis for these privileges is either eroded or no longer exists. As a loving critic of local church strategies, I find little evidence that long-range plans include intentional action to address the systemic sins of the surrounding culture. To salve our conscience we adopt a bandwagon cause for relief of victims but avoid the grit of social, political, and economic action to change the system. Of course, we use the excuse that the social gospel of liberal Christianity proved to be a colossal failure, but that doesn't fly in the face of the fact that Jesus came to right the wrongs of injustice as well as to redeem us from our sins. Ray Bakke is known as a global urbanologist with a passion

3. Quoted in Colson, *The Body*, 73.

for the poor and the needs of the city. In his book, *A Theology as Big as the City*, Bakke takes us deeply into his heart and mind as he confesses, "The burden of my life has been to find a suitable spirituality for urban ministry."[4] Confronting the inevitable tensions among Scripture, history, church, and city, he finds balance in Scripture as the final test of "doing theology" in the context of the city. What a contrast with the recommendation of a strategic planning consultant hired at a high eate by a local church in the city of Las Vegas. His final report came back calling for the gimmicks of a branding logo and theme song.

I believe that Jesus has a mediating institution in mind when he prays for oneness "so that the world may believe that you have sent me" (John 17:20–21). As much as he believes in the kind of association that he has with his disciples and the kind of movement that he promises at Pentecost, he also knows that it will take the focused energy of a social institution to change the culture at its core. No magic is needed to describe the institution he had in mind. Using the model advanced by Andy Crouch in his book *Playing God: Redeeming the Gift of Power*, the institutional church would have the sacraments of baptism and communion as its artifacts, a multi-generational community as its market, a discipline of character leading to holiness for its members, and a description of roles based upon gifts of the Spirit.[5] Crouch also reminds us that it takes at least three generations for a mediating institution to develop, only one generation for it to fall from prime, and less than one generation for it to be corrupted to the core. Everything depends upon the oneness of leadership in relationship with the Father and the Son.

So, like ancient Israelites planting an olive tree, Christians are called to lead institutions that are designed for the future. Thomas Friedman posed the same question in the title of his book *The Lexus and the Olive Tree*.[6] Our gift of succession for organizational accord can be a sleek new Lexus that will soon wear out and become obsolete, or our legacy can be a gnarly old olive tree that will sustain the faith in future generations. Jesus has the olive tree in mind.

4. Bakke, *A Theology as Big as the City*, 203.

5. Crouch, *Playing God*, 178.

6. T. Friedman, *The Lexus and the Olive Tree*, 474–75.

12

The Gift of *Agape*

"I have made you known to them,
and will continue to make you known to them
in order that the love you have for me may be in them
and that I myself may be in them."

(JOHN 17:26)

WHAT IS THE ULTIMATE gift that a leader can leave to a successor? Jesus concludes the Prayer of Succession by asking again that his disciples might be as one in the love that he and his Father knew in their earthly as well as their eternal relationship. This love is the bond that makes oneness possible among the disciples and in the church. Yes, it is genuine affection for each other in every relationship, but so much more. Pointedly, Jesus uses the word *agape,* meaning "sacrificial love," as the defining characteristic of the Father's relationship with him, his relationship with the Father, his relationship with us, and our relationship with him. It is also the defining characteristic for the body of Christ in concert as his church and all of its representative ministries. By personal example and organizational ethos, sacrificial love is the greatest gift that we can leave for our successors.

Sacrificial love is the Father so loving the world that he gave his Son, the Son so loving the Father that he would do nothing by himself, and his disciples so loving their Lord that they are willing to die for him. We speak these truths by creed, but it is quite different to test them at the ground level where they really count. After a lifetime of service in Christian institutions of higher education, the reflective years of retirement have taught me that I have barely scratched the surface of the meaning of sacrificial love. Like a deep-sea diver, the Spirit of God has taken me down into the depths of my faith until I have almost touched bottom. There the exploration continues.

The Discipline of Daily Death

Call me an "AA Christian." Like a member of Alcoholics Anonymous, I begin each day before getting out of bed by making the vow, "This day I die. . ."—a highly personalized list of specifics completes the sentence. Not only do I vow, "This day I die to self," but I name the temptations that can trip up my soul, especially the signature sin or sins to which I am most vulnerable. Once I pronounce the death sentence on each of them, I then claim God's power of resurrection as I rise and say, "This day I come alive in Christ . . . to think his thoughts, show his spirit, and do his work." Even at the age of eighty-five, I find that every day becomes an adventure as God opens up "ministry moments" with people on the street, friends from the past, needs of neighbors, and consultation with colleagues. "This day I rise with Christ . . ." is a sure antidote for the ailments of aging and doldrums of depression. Eugene Peterson's *The Message* translation of "Abba Father" (Rom 8:15) as "What's next, Papa?" voices my anticipation for each new day in his good will. Now when I sign my letters, "With His joy," I really mean it.

Again, it would be a mistake to assume that I have arrived. The discipline of daily death is dangerous because it opens us to the deep probes of the Holy Spirit who takes us down one level at a time until we reach the bedrock of our faith. It is there that we learn from experience the ultimate meaning of sacrificial love.

Surrender Without Stipulation

Surrender is a militant word that goes against the grain of a generation that has cancelled out the hymn "Onward Christian Soldiers." We prefer to talk about making a commitment to Christ, putting our trust in him, or accepting him as our Savior. In each case, the initiative belongs to us and the decision sounds as if we are doing Christ a favor. We surrender, but the control remains in our hands.

Jesus' first question to Peter at their breakfast meeting after the resurrection was, "Simon, son of John, do you truly love me more than these?" (John 21:18). We can envision Jesus looking down at Peter's fishing gear on the ground as he spoke. From earlier in the Gospels, we already know that Peter is a control freak. With the crucifixion and burial of Christ, Peter had seen everything spin out of control. His natural response was to go back to fishing, the occupation in which he was competent and comfortable. The fishing gear on the ground symbolized his loss of faith and his need to regain control.

Peter's response is not strange to us. Christian leaders, especially those in top positions of command and control, are particularly susceptible to surrender with stipulation. Having run our little worlds, we assume that God cannot get along without our hands on the controls. As a student pilot during my high school days, I was shooting landings in a little Piper J-3 with my instructor in the seat behind. When I came in too hot and too hard, the airplane hit the ground, bounced up, and just hung there. I felt the throttle ripped out of my hand, the engine thrust to full power, and the airplane flung into the sky again. An angry instructor then shouted over the intercom, "If I had left the controls in your hand you would have crashed us!" The lesson has come back to me time and time again, especially when I assumed a college presidency. I had to learn the difference between self-control, a virtue for leadership, and self in control, a vice of leadership. When Dan Evans, governor of the state of Washington, was under pressure to run for the United State Senate as our junior senator, he confessed to me, "Once you have been number one, it is hard to start over."

The governor's words help explain why the story of Peter has an extra bite in it for Christian leaders. After Jesus asks three times, "Do you love me?" and Peter answers with passionate affirmation each time, the Lord puts his answers to the ultimate test with the command, "Follow me" (John 21:15–19). True to form as a control freak, Peter takes a few steps forward, stops, look back at John, and pleads, "What about him?" (John 21:21). Surrender, even to the death, came with the stipulation that Peter would keep his penchant to be in control always.

Jesus counters with a statement that I have heard many times during my retirement years. After spending thirty-three years as a college, university, and seminary president, plus multiple leadership positions in religious, educational, and civic associations, it is natural for me to track the direction, policies, and practices of the current and emerging generations. But, every time I am tempted to run the world by asking the question, "What about him?" the resounding answer is "What is that to you? You must follow me"(John 21:22). Christ is asking for full surrender without stipulation.

While learning this painful lesson, I discovered a deeper truth that upset all of my preconceptions about surrender without stipulation. In the book *All In*, Mark Batterson tells the story of nineteenth-century missionaries who answered God's call by putting all of their possessions into a casket and buying a one-way ticket to the mission field.[1] This was a level of surrender that I had never known. Even when answering God's call to work in India or to Christian higher education, I always had the assurance of a supoort system—my church, my family, my education, my youth—in case it didn't work out. While I don't recall making stipulations with my surrender to do the full will of God, the case had never really been tested. The closest I came to putting all our possessions in a casket and buying a one-way ticket to answer the call of God came with a financial crisis that threatened the viability and reputation of the institution to which I had just been elected president. We had just moved across the country with a young family of four children, including a five-week-old baby, when I learned that the institution's line of credit was exhausted, the tactic of juggling debts had run its course, and until tuition revenues came in for the fall enrollment there were no funds to meet the August payroll. Under the threat of potential bankruptcy, I took my wife to lunch. As always, I laid out options. I said, "We have every reason to resign because the facts were not known at the time of our election. Or we can stay and work for recovery. We may fail, and who wants a failure for a president? One thing is sure, I will not lose either you or our family." Jan, who sacrificed the most in making our move, listened patiently and then calmly asked, "Do you believe that God called us to this position?" When I answered, "Yes," she gave our marching orders: "What are we waiting for? Let's get going." I guarantee that it was the women in the missionary story who got the caskets, packed their possessions in them, and bought the one-way tickets.

Jesus is our example of surrender without stipulation. Time and again he takes himself out of the picture in deference to his Father:

> I tell you the truth, the Son can do nothing by himself; he can do
> only what he sees his Father doing, because whatever the Father
> does the Son also does (John 5:19).

1. Batterson, *All In*, 13ff.

By myself I can do nothing; I judge only as I hear, and my judgment is just, for I seek not to please myself but him who sent me (John 5:30).

He who speaks on his own does so to gain honor for himself, but he who works for the honor of the one who sent him is a man of truth; there is nothing false about him (John 7:18).

For I did not speak of my own accord, but the Father who sent me commanded me what to say and how to say it. I know that his command leads to eternal life. So whatever I say is just what the Father has told me to say (John 12:49–50).

I will not speak with you much longer, for the prince of this world is coming. He has no hold on me, but the world must learn that I love the Father and that I do exactly what my Father has commanded me (John 14:31).

With these words, Jesus drives a stake right through the heart of the contemporary mind-set. For a full generation now, radical self-interest has reigned supreme. Back in the 1980s, we were introduced to Sheila, who said, "I am my own religion."[2] Today, in the world of social media, *selfie* is the word most often tweeted (used on Twitter). Radical individualism no longer hides in the closet behind the false face of altruism. It has "come out" as its own god, self-contained and self-controlled. Anyone who relies on sources outside the immanent self, especially a Christian who bows before a transcendent God, is spurned as weak and cowardly. Why should we be surprised? Choosing the weakest and most helpless of creatures, Isaiah predicted, "he was led like a lamb to the slaughter, and as a sheep before her shearers is silent, so he did not open his mouth" (Isa 53:7). Peter, a firsthand witness to the fulfillment of this prophecy, wrote, "When they hurled their insults at him, he did not retaliate; when he suffered, he made no threats. Instead, he entrusted himself to him who judges justly" (1 Pet 2:23). Yes, there is a high price to be paid for surrender without stipulation, but when Christ commands, "Follow me," he challenges the charge of critics who mistake obedience for weakness.

2. Bellah et al., *Habits of the Heart*, 221.

Sacrifice Without Success

A Christian leader is, first and foremost, a servant. Secular leadership literature is to be credited for adopting the term "servant-leader" with its implications for personal humility and interpersonal responsibility for serving others. Jesus, while accepting this meaning of servanthood, adds another dimension when he announces, "The Son of Man came not to be served, but to serve and give his life as a ransom for many" (Matt 20:28). Once again, those of us who claim to be servant-leaders in the name of Christ are confronted by the dual challenge of faithful stewardship and sacrificial love. Faithful stewardship is to serve others rather than ourselves; sacrificial love is to die for others rather than live for ourselves. Few of us are called to sacrifice our lives in our love for others, but all of us are called to be faithful in selfless service to others. But what if we are called to be faithful stewards without ever seeing the evidence of success? The question puts us on a collision course with the highest value of our contemporary age. As I pointed out in my book *Christ-Centered Leadership: The Incarnational Difference*, success is the secular standard by which our performance is judged, not just in the eyes of the world, but all too often in the eyes of the church. Anything less than the tangible and measurable results of success are deemed to be a failure.[3] To reinforce this outlook, we reward success with awards for achievement, honors for outcomes, and celebrity status for stars of the media or the marketplace. Faithful stewardship and sacrificial love are seldom recognized unless we can also find some element of success attached to them. Even in our Christian colleges, universities, and seminaries we choose our distinguished alumni on the basis of their achievements. Would we ever dare to give honor to a person in the religious or secular world who lived out the meaning of "good and faithful servant" without some evidence of success? Would we ever have the courage to establish an "Alumni Hall of Fame" with election based upon the Scripture, "These were all commended for their faith, yet none of them received what had been promised"? (Heb 11:39). The honorees would join the likes of Abraham, Isaac, Jacob, Joseph, Moses, Rahab, Gideon, David, Samuel, and Jesus, who would be judged as failures according to contemporary standards.

Self-esteem is the issue at stake. It is a natural drive that Satan exploits in order to damn us. If he can get us to equate success with self-esteem, he gains the leverage of pride as the sin that derails us. Earlier, I told the story

---

3. McKenna, *Christ-Centered Leadership*, 21.

about the battle of wills that I had with the Spirit of God over my plans for the PhD and my call to India. Even though I put no stipulation on my surrender, a skeptic might say that the story came out my way because I achieved the PhD, served in Christian higher education for forty-one years, and never made it to India. But what if it hadn't worked out that way? What if I gave those forty-one years to faithful ministry without tangible success? Would my life have been a failure?

The answer comes in another story. James Hudson Taylor III, grandson of Hudson Taylor, the nineteenth-century missionary statesman to China, and I were best friends in college and seminary. After graduation from seminary, James returned to China and followed in the path of his grandfather as executive director of Oriental Mission Fellowship (formerly China Inland Mission). In further preparation for his leadership role, he enrolled in the PhD program at Yale University. After completing his M.A. in Chinese history, he received an urgent call from China reporting a crisis in OMF that desperately needed his leadership in order to avoid organizational disaster. Without a question, James reversed all systems, took a leave from Yale, and moved his family back to China. He never returned to Yale or completed the PhD. Faithful to his calling, he gave the rest of his life in executive leadership of missions in China. Knowing the inside story, I exercised my presidential prerogative at Asbury Theological Seminary by successfully nominating him to our faculty and board for an honorary doctorate at commencement in 1991. Ten years later, while serving as chair of the board of trustees at Spring Arbor University (also Taylor's alma mater), I knew of James's battle with cancer and again recommended him to receive an honorary doctorate at commencement. Cancer, however, spread rapidly through his system and he could not make the trip back to the United States. In response, the board authorized President Charles Webb to confer the degree upon James with full regalia in his Hong Kong hospital room. James Hudson Taylor III is remembered as the man who sacrificed the prestige of a Yale PhD in order to serve the needs of the Chinese people. Academic success in traditional terms may have eluded him, but if you ask missionaries to China or the Chinese people themselves, they will tell you that faithful stewardship and sacrificial love earned him the title of "Dr. Taylor" and the reputation as one of the great missionary statesmen of the twentieth century.

Suffering Without Support

Suffering is inseparable from sacrificial love. Pain may come from family and friends who do not understand our decision to do the will of God. When I accepted the call to Asbury Theological Seminary and moved from Seattle Pacific University, my colleagues in Christian higher education warned that I was "riding off into the sunset." Other pain may come from the fatigue due to the stress of 24/7 leadership. In my own career, I learned to read the early signs of physical exhaustion. When I found myself lacking clarity for understanding issues, losing patience with staff members, or hesitating to make obvious decisions, I knew that I needed a break.

Depression is a frequent form of suffering for leaders. Winston Churchill battled what he called the "black dog of depression," and Abraham Lincoln suffered so much from its effects that he wrote, "I am now the most miserable man living."[4] Other leaders whom we extol have admitted the same dark cloud over their souls during their private moments. Whether depression comes from the inherited weakness of bipolar swings or from the highs and lows of the institutional cycle, the fact remains: leaders, whether in secular or religious professions, are especially vulnerable to depression.

Doubt can also be a special form of suffering for leaders, even Christian leaders. Mother Teresa had the adulation of Christians and non-Christians across the world for her sacrificial love given to hopeless people in the slums of Calcutta. Sainthood seemed assured for her. During the investigation for sainthood, however, letters were found with the confession of "hidden darkness" in her soul and the conclusion, "If I become a saint, I will surely be one of darkness. I will continually be absent from heaven—to [light] the light of those in darkness on earth."[5]

The most pain comes, however, when our mortality is threatened. In 1987, a regular physical examination led the doctor to assess my family history of heart disease, my high-stress position trying to resolve internal organizational conflict, and my symptoms of high blood pressure, high cholesterol, and irregular heartbeat. The diagnosis served as a wake-up call for my health and my survival. I realized then how much I was driven by the will to live and the need for self-preservation. The experience took me back to Jesus' temptation to turn the stones into bread in order to survive

4. *60 Minutes.*

5. Kolodiejchuk, *Mother Teresa,* 230.

in the wilderness and then forward to his final prayer in the garden of Gethsemane, where he prayed, "Let this cup pass from me" (Mark 14:36). His last temptation is not his love for Mary Magdalene, as proposed by a novelist, but his love for life itself. We share that love in our will to live and in our drive for self-preservation. Suffering, whether spiritual, psychological, or physical, tests our faith at the ground level. For one thing, suffering introduces us to the reality that we need help. Leaders are expected to be self-sufficient. To admit that we need help is a threat to that confidence. Andy Crouch, in his book *Playing God*, reminds us that we are born totally "disabled" and will die totally "disabled." In between birth and death we are "temporarily abled," but often act as if it is a permanent condition.[6]

Few of us know what it means to suffer without a support system to comfort, relieve, and heal us. We count on family and friends, pastors and physicians, counselors and therapists to rally around us in our time of need. But what if we were called to suffer without a support system? Job's plight is the classic example. Condemned by his best friends as a sinner, he screams into God's silence. All support systems fall away and Job is left alone with the reality of his helplessness. When God finally speaks out of the whirlwind, Job can only say, "I shut my mouth" (Job 40:4). Ultimately, God honors his screaming protest, dogged resolution, and humble confession by doubling all of the blessings that he had lost, but the torturous path that led him to that moment cannot be forgotten.

Add to Job's suffering the most painful moments ever experienced by a human being when Jesus cried from the cross, "My God, My God, why have You forsaken me?"(Matt 27:46). No one has ever suffered so much or been so totally abandoned. Satan's final weapon is death, with the silence of God. The closest I have come to feeling the pain of loneliness that Jesus must have suffered comes from reading Francois Mauriac's foreword to Elie Wiesel's book *Night*. Mauriac is a Christian theologian responding to Wiesel's recollection of being a twelve-year-old Jewish boy seeing another little boy with the "sad face of angel"being hung by the Nazis at Auschwitz. Wiesel hears a voice behind him groan, "Where is God? Where is He? Where can He be now?" Within his own child's heart, Wiesel answers, "Where? Here he is—he has been hanged here, on these gallows."[7]

What can a Christian say to a Jew who has lost his faith? Mauriac asks, "Did I speak of the other Jew, his brother, who may have resembled

6. Crouch, *Playing God*, 268.
7. Wiesel, *Night*, xvii ff.

him—the Crucified, whose Cross has conquered the world? Did I affirm that the stumbling block to his faith was the cornerstone of mine?" Mauriac's search for a word of comfort continues as he considers the resurrection of Zion, the all-pervasive presence of grace, and the fact that the eternal God will have the last word. Finally, he concedes, "This is what I could have told the Jewish child. But I could only embrace him, weeping."[8]

Philip Yancey takes up the same question in his book *The Question That Won't Go Away*. Whether it is Jesus on the cross, Wiesel in a concentration camp, or parents of children who die in the Newtown massacre, there are no easy answers to those who suffer when God seems silent. Like us, Yancey succumbs to the question. "As I stood there with tears streaming down my face, I had no idea what to say. So we just stood there, holding hands . . ."[9]

C. S. Lewis also grapples with the most difficult of all questions in his essay "The Efficacy of Prayer." He asks, "Does God then forsake just those who serve Him best? Well, He who served Him best of all said, near His tortured death, 'Why hast Thou forsaken Me?'" Lewis's conclusion shatters all of our easy expectations for answered prayer. "If we were braver, we might be sent, with far less help, to defend far more desperate outposts in the great battle."[10]

To suffer death when God is silent is the rock bottom of our faith. It is the deepest we can go. But what do we find when we get there? Arthur John Gossip, a peerless Scottish preacher, helps us in his sermon "But When Life Tumbles In, What Then?" He preached this sermon on a Sunday in 1927, the day after his wife collapsed and died. At first he thought that he could not speak because of his grief. Then he realized that this was the time to speak because his faith was being tested and his congregation needed to hear how he would respond. After reviewing the stages of grief and the magnitude of his lost love, he concludes, "What can separate us from His love? . . . No, not death, for standing in the roaring of the Jordan, cold with its dreadful chill, very conscious of its terror, of it rushing, I, too, like Hopeful in *Pilgrim's Progress*, can call back to you who one day in your turn will have to cross it, 'Be of good cheer, my brother, for I feel the bottom and it is sound.'" While Gossip leaves no doubt about the surety of God's presence at the time of death, he does not forget those moments when we are all alone,

8. Ibid.

9. Yancey, *The Question that Never Goes Away*, 122.

10. Lewis, "The Efficacy of Prayer," 10–11.

in the dark, and God's voice is silent. For those times, he also writes, "You people in the sunshine may believe the faith, but we in the shadow must believe it. We have nothing else."[11]

So, after exploring many gifts of succession, we conclude that of all these gifts—authority, anointing, accountability, anticipation, administration, and accord—the greatest of these is *agape*, or sacrificial love, that may ask us to suffer death in the silence of God with only the assurance of his unseen presence and the certainty of his promised resurrection.

Sacrificial love is the gritty essence of our Christian witness in the world, personally and corporately. We are called to pass on to our successor the evidence of sacrificial love in our personal leadership and we are charged with the responsibility to show evidence of that same spirit in the ethos of the organization we are called to lead. Honesty prompts us to confess that we have fallen short on both counts. If we ask the "man on the street" the question, "Does sacrificial love set apart Christian leaders and the Christian church in our society today?" what answer will we get?

In finality, we have to weigh Christian leadership on the scale of sacrificial love. As deficient as we may be, the ideal cannot be compromised. Christ expects us to demonstrate as persons and infuse as leaders the word and the spirit of sacrificial love. No gift of succession is more costly or more effective. If we are true to our trust, the gift of *agape*, spelled out in the evidence of sacrificial love as seen in us and in the organization we lead, will ultimately define the character of our leadership. The greatest gift we can give to our successor is the gift of sacrificial love.

Postscript

At 3:30 p.m. on Thursday, June 5, 2014 I was at my computer writing this chapter when I heard Jan's urgent call: "Honey, there has been a shooting at Seattle Pacific University." Rushing to the TV in the family room, we sat together holding hands and watching a surrealistic scene unfold before our eyes. News cameras on the ground and in the air zeroed in on the Otto Miller Science Center, a campus building whose name and history carried a wealth of memories for us. Otto Miller had just retired as professor of physics when we arrived on campus to assume the presidency in 1968. A white-haired giant and Christian gentleman with a ramrod for a spine and

11. Gossip, "But When Life Tumbles In, What Then?," in Blackwood, ed., *The Protestant Pulpit*, 204, 201.

a smile that instantly disarmed you, he left no doubt whose name would appear on our new science center. The choice of the word "new" may be a bit misleading because the Otto Miller Science Center was really a recycled trolley barn on the south shore of the Washington Ship Canal. Just hearing Otto's name and seeing his building brought back a rush of memories while we waited for the full story of the shooting to unfold.

When we became the presidential couple at Seattle Pacific College in 1968, we stepped into leadership for a Christian college located in the center of a burgeoning city. As a student in the field of higher education, I scoped out the scene and made some observations as background for my leadership. In contrast with the typical Christian college located in a village or suburb where community was created by social pressure, the campus and the curriculum of SPC tended to take on the character of its urban location and diverse population. Even though the college claimed "community," faculty and students seldom came together, except at basketball games and commencement. Chapel was split into three separately meeting segments; athletic teams and musical and drama groups were silos of specialization; residence halls had their own individualized imprint; the curriculum was a cafeteria of choices without a core in the Christian liberal arts; Spiritual Emphasis Week attracted only a fraction of the campus population; and students could escape into urban anonymity just a block away from campus. Yet, just under the surface of the splinters, the history and theology and spirit of the college continued as a latent bond for the faculty, students, and alumni.

In response to this challenge, my vision for presidential leadership began with the theme "A Vision of Wholeness." Chapel talks centering on the theological and educational concepts of wholeness were scheduled throughout my first year. Then I took responsibility for chapel as "The President's Course," rented the Free Methodist Church across from the campus, and brought the three chapels together in one "community" service. Under the same theme of wholeness, I proposed curricular reform in the core requirements for courses in the Christian liberal arts. Looking over the campus map, I saw the older buildings of the lower campus united by the beloved "Loop," but no connecting link bringing the newer buildings of the upper campus together with a spatial center. So, when financial resources permitted us to buy the old trolley barn along the canal and recycle it as the Otto Miller Science Center, we had our first chance to put the idea of wholeness into architectural design. Recycling and environmental concerns were the mode of the day so we installed heat pumps to bring in water from the ship canal for heating and cooling, designed open modules for offices and labs, and even approached the National Science Foundation for a grant to experiment with solar energy. Our proposal was rejected by the NSF with a gentle gibe because Seattle had sunshine only 28 percent of the year and, at the time, there was no way to store the energy for future use. When we turned our attention to the front and center of the building, we had to deal with a turntable for bringing train engines in for repairs and a deep pit for mechanics to work on their underbellies. It became the perfect spot to introduce into a scientific facility the circle of "humanizing" space. So, rather than filling the pit and covering the floor, we recycled the turntable as an open amphitheater for lounging, study, lectures, and receptions with the added feature of artistic wall hangings to soften the space. In the Otto Miller Science Center, we were ready for community.

All of these thoughts came back to me on the day of the shooting. Along with the memories came the dash of reality. To think of this work of love that represented the best planning of our faculty and full funding by our community being violated by a fatal shooting overwhelmed us emotionally. Shock wave after shock wave came with each bit of unfolding news—two shooters, six gurneys, one dead, and hundreds of students in lockdown. But then, another story started leaking through. An articulate eyewitness transfixed the media with her description of the event and the daring actions of her fellow students. Another camera focused on groups of students huddling on the street and holding each other in prayer on the campus lawn. The student monitor of the building was escorted to a gurney, loaded into an emergency vehicle, and taken to the hospital. The mayor of Seattle expressed official concern and the president of the university adroitly handled tough questions but choked up at mention of the victims. It was then that the pace of the turtle took on the speed of the hare. Story after story of sacrifice, togetherness, and community resulted in a rush that not even the secular media could ignore. In the worldwide network of corporate media and through the ubiquitous influence of social media, sacrificial love defined the Seattle Pacific University community and, as when E. F. Hutton speaks, everyone paid attention.

I learned my lesson. Try as we might to create community out of visions, slogans, policy, programs, and even buildings, it does not happen until sacrificial love reveals itself as the personal bond that brings us together in humility and in faith. In my daybook for June 5, 2014, I paraphrased the words of an old Jewish legend: "God looked down on Seattle Pacific University today and said, "Here is where love meets; here I will build My community." Or, even better said, on this day at Seattle Pacific University Jesus' Prayer of Succession was answered, "May they be brought to complete unity to let the world know that you sent me and have loved them even as you have loved me" (John 17:23). Sacrificial love still wins the world.

13

The Succession Package: "Seamless Transition"

WHAT HAVE WE LEARNED about succession in Christian leadership? On the baseline of Succession Principles, our boards and leaders are no different than our counterparts in secular organizations. Common expectations include:

1. Christian leadership shares the *standards of good practices* for succession with all organizations. Succession planning is an integral part of our executive responsibility and incumbent leaders must foresee the legacy that they will pass on to their successors. Christian leadership is not exempt from the standard requirements for succession, such as the transfer of organizational vision, mission, and tone along with the integrity of title and task and proven procedures for good transition.

2. Christian leadership jointly recognizes that succession is a *comprehensive package*. Our tendency is to segregate the expectations of character for the selection of leaders, competence for the service of leaders, and continuity for the succession of leaders into separate packages. Leadership theory shows us that these expectations are interlinked like a seamless garment and predictive of leadership at its best.

3. Christian leadership is also a *process* as well as a plan. Boards tend to think of a succession as a plan to be executed when an executive is ready to retire or move on. Perhaps there is the fear that thinking of succession any earlier might cast doubt on the security of the incumbent leader. This is a faulty viewpoint because the line of succession

not only runs from leader to leader but also from stage to stage in leadership development. A succession plan adopted during the final stage of leadership often focuses on role and functions, discusses internal and external candidates, and uses the boilerplate selection process of executive search firms. Consequently, the board's primary responsibility to preserve and advance the mission of the organization is drawn as a dotted line of persons rather than a solid line of purpose. Long before the time when our boards have to ask, "What is our succession plan?" we should be asking, "What is our succession process?" Through the seamless garment of succession we need to see the continuous thread of leadership development.

Spiritual Principles of Succession

From this point on, our view of succession in Christian leadership takes on special meaning. Our thinking must break through the plane of standard expectations to a transcendent level. Christian leadership has the solemn responsibility of eternal purpose. As Christ counts upon his Father's trust, truth, and love in the development of his disciples, we too must put spiritual leadership at the top of our organizational agenda with succession in mind. When we make this commitment, we draw upon the understandings we have gained from the study of succession through the prayer, teaching, and modeling of Jesus Christ.

Succession Transfers Assets

Christian leadership gives *priority* to the assets transferred from one generation to another according to the Succession Principle:

> What we bring to our leadership is *important;*
> What we do in our leadership is *more important;*
> What we leave from our leadership is *most important of all.*

Implicit in this statement is the shift in thinking from the secular goal of success to the spiritual goal of succession. In the triad we see that succession is a full-circle process involving character in selection, competence in service, and continuity in succession. Furthermore, the Succession Principle reorders the priorities for leadership development. Mission takes priority over position, relationships take priority over achievements, and long-term goals take priority over short-term gains. Because the sustainability of organizations depends on the continuity of leadership in each new generation, what we leave from our leadership to our successor is most important of all.

Succession Is a Paradox

Succession in Christian leadership is a *paradox*. As Max De Pree reminds us in his book *Leadership Is an Art*, every leader is a servant and a debtor.[1] Our debt begins with the primary responsibility for passing to a successor the physical, financial, and organizational assets that are entrusted to us. Our obligation then rises to the level of moral integrity and relational responsibility required of all leaders. At this point, Christ breaks the plane of the natural world in the Prayer of Succession by adding the debt of spiritual maturity to the expectations for those who follow him.

How then can the debt of a leader become a gift to a successor? How can the onus of an obligation give way to the freedom of a celebration? The answer comes back as a paradox of truth: A Christian leader carries the legacy received from his or her predecessor as a debt to be paid until it is passed on as a gift to the successor. At this point it becomes a debt of the new leader and a potential gift to the next successor. In this paradox, the line of succession is assured from generation to generation.

Succession Accomplishes God's Grand Design

Succession in Christian leadership is essential to accomplish *God's grand design for human redemption*. As the Father gives Jesus all power for the singular and ultimate purpose of bringing eternal life to all people, Christian leaders must never lose sight of the same goal. In management terms, human sin is the problem that gives Christian leaders our strategic challenge, meaningful mission, and ultimate purpose. Unless our leadership is driven by the desire to bring eternal life to all people, we cannot justify our existence. Take heed, leaders of Christian educational institutions, relief ministries, humanitarian organizations, and even evangelical denominations: our penultimate purpose can never become an end in itself. On a

---

1. De Pree, *Leadership Is an Art*, 11.

regular basis our organizational boards and leaders need to stop and ask, "What is our mission?" After answering that question, we need to stop again to answer the question behind the question: "How then does our mission contribute to the Father's purpose of bringing eternal life to all people?"

Succession Is a Sacred Trust

Succession in Christian leadership is a *sacred trust* for preserving and advancing God's investment in us. We readily understand how God the Father gives his Son all power, all truth, and all love to accomplish his assigned task in the plan of redemption. It is mind-boggling, however, to think that these same legacies are entrusted in us as Christian leaders. No greater trust can come to us. The legacies given by the Father to his Son and passed on to us define the essence of Christian leadership. Our sacred trust is to exercise the power, teach the truth, and demonstrate the love that God the Father has entrusted to us through his Son.

The Christian Leader as Role Player

In the line of succession a Christian leader is only a *role player* in the unfolding drama of God's redemptive mission. Even though our salvation depends solely upon Jesus' role in God's plan for human redemption, he never sees himself as the only actor. Yes, his sacrifice is the denouement of the drama, but it is not the end of the story. Each of us has a role to play, but always remember that the story does not begin or end with us. Whether our part is large or small, we must never forget that we are in the line of succession for an unfolding story that will never end until Jesus comes again. In this role, we find meaning because it puts us personally with Jesus Christ into the strategic challenge of bringing eternal life to all people.

A Leader's Specific Tasks

In the line of succession every Christian leader is given a *specific task* to be completed within the limits of a career and a lifetime. Although every Christian leader has to learn the dance of multitasking, we cannot lose sight of our primary task. It is to develop mature disciples who are ready to step into the role of leadership. This assigned task complements the strategic role of a Christian leader with a tactical process. An organic structure activated by synchronized functions aims at completion and closure. Along with Jesus, we must accept the fact that our role as a leader will come to an end, our task will be finished, and we will have to give an accounting to the Father for the task assigned to us.

Succession and Spiritually Mature Followers

Succession in Christian leadership comes to its crux in the task of developing *spiritually mature followers* who are shaped by the word of truth and prepared to take on the leader's role and the specific task for their generation. In a nutshell, the primary task of a Christian leader is to make Christian leaders. To qualify for this role and task, we and our followers must show the same spiritual maturity that Jesus developed in his disciples—internalized truth, unshakable confidence, unconditional joy, and disciplined holiness.

Finishing Strong and Closing Well

Succession in Christian leadership depends upon *finishing strong and closing well*. We must finish strong to assure the line of succession and we must close well to complete our assigned task in God's redemptive plan. The Apostle Paul follows this plan in his final charge to Timothy. Passing on his leadership role, he writes, "I give you this charge: Preach the Word. . . . Do the work of an evangelist, discharge all the duties of your ministry" (2 Tim 4:2–5). With equal precision, he comes to closure on his task: "For I am already being poured out like a drink offering, and the time has come for my departure. I have fought the good fight, I have finished the race, I have kept the faith" (2 Tim 4:6–7). His words of valediction set the standard for us. Our role as Christian leaders will be judged by *continuity* and our task will be judged by *completion*.

The Unity of Sacrificial Love

Succession in Christian leadership stretches forward to see the *unity* of sacrificial love demonstrated in the cooperative associations of the body of

Christ and the mediating institutions of the church of Jesus Christ as our indisputable witness in the world.

The Gift of Greater Things

Succession is complete when Christian leaders who follow us see the *gift of greater things* in bringing eternal life to all people. Our legacy will be written not in the good things that we have done as Christian leaders, but in the greater things that our successor will do. While seeing this vision, we do not prescribe it. Our task is to share the legacy of Christ by exercising our authority, completing our task, accepting our responsibility, and giving the glory to God. Then, as we and our followers are true to his trust, transformed by his truth, and unified in his love, the promise of Jesus to Nathanael will come to us: "You shall see greater things . . ." (John 1:50).

Hubris gives way to humility when we read and reflect upon these ten foundational truths derived directly from the final report of Jesus Christ to his Father. Can we measure up? Self-awareness shows us our shortfall. Succession in Christian leadership puts a white-hot light on the fact that we cannot depend upon human resources to achieve God's purpose. With evidence of our utter dependence upon him, the message will be clear to all those who follow us. We have not arrived, but we are on the way. This is the debt of love as well as the gift of grace that we leave our successor. God is still willing to take a chance on maturing people in the fellowship of love. With confidence, then, we can turn our attention to the final question, "What do I leave my successor?"

EPILOGUE

The Succession Speech:
"The Gift of Greater Things"

IMAGINE THAT YOU, AS a Christian leader, are invited to speak at the introduction of your successor. What will you say?

When I ask myself this question, I am instantly drawn back to the final report of Jesus to his Father in John 17. Feeling as deeply into the mind and heart of Jesus as I can, I recall that the Father's investment of trust, truth, and love in his Son was also bequeathed to me through the line of succession when I answered the call to Christian leadership. With these legacies comes the debt I owe to pass them on, intact and enhanced, as gifts to my successor. In this spirit, I offer the following speech:

The Gift of Greater Things

Thank you for the honor of giving a speech that will say "farewell" and "welcome" at the same time. To say "farewell" I might call to memory some of the accomplishments of my administration; to say "welcome" I might look ahead and offer some advice to my successor. I will do neither. Rather, I choose to remember the legacy of leadership given to Jesus Christ from his Father and transferred to me as his disciple. The best way I know how to say "farewell" as your past leader and say "welcome" to you, my successor, is to recall the gifts entrusted to me, accept my responsibility for them, and pass them on.

The Legacy of Trust

Jesus opens his final report to his Father by acknowledging that the time has come for him to account for the authority entrusted to him to lead with purpose, manage the resources given to him, and complete his assigned task. I, too, have come to that time and must also give an accounting for the legacy of trust that Christ has put in me. As best I know, I have been true to my trust and pass on to you these gifts of succession:

—*I leave you the gift of authority granted to me by Christ and exercised only to advance the Father's purpose of bringing eternal life to all people, never for personal or political advantage;*

—*I leave you the gift of accomplishment with the evidence that I have completed my assigned task and pass on to you an organic structure and a synchronized system of management upon which you can build;*

—*I leave you the gift of accountability for the development of maturing leaders who will advance the Father's purpose, complete their assigned task, pass on their legacy to their successors, and give the glory to God.*

These three gifts—authority, accomplishment, and accountability—based upon the legacy of trust given to us by Christ and passed on through the line of succession are the credentials that a Christian brings to leadership. With these gifts, we have all of the resources we need to bring our followers to maturity for leadership, through whom succession will continue.

The Legacy of Truth

As the character of Jesus was shaped by his unswerving obedience to the word of the Father, we too are given the legacy of truth to develop the spiritual qualities that define the Christian leader. Again, without claiming perfection for myself or my followers, I owe you, as my successor, the legacy of truth in gifts:

—*I leave you the gift of acceptance by which the word of truth is so thoroughly embraced by those whom I lead that they are ready to communicate it to others as their very own;*

—*I leave you the gift of assurance with the name of the Father and the Son imprinted as the personal identity, divine protection, and unshakable confidence in those whom I am entrusted to lead;*

—I leave you the gift of affirmation in followers who know the complete joy of Jesus Christ, given in obedience to the word of truth, and independent of circumstances;

—I leave you the gift of anointing by the personal example of submitting myself to the word of truth in order that our followers may also be made holy, set apart and anointed by the Holy Spirit.

As Jesus was willing to gamble the Father's redemptive purpose on the qualifications of his disciples, we too depend upon the maturity of our followers to continue the work after we have finished strong and closed well. For you, my successor, I leave you a maturing team of leaders whose competence, character, and compassion reflect the image of Jesus Christ himself.

The Legacy of Love

Confident that the legacy of trust for the calling and the legacy of truth for the character of his disciples will continue from generation to generation, Jesus anticipates the fulfillment of the Great Commission through a line of succession that will extend forward until the Father's redemptive purpose is complete. His optimism is found in the legacy of love that will define the body of Christ through the institution of his church.

—I leave you the gift of anticipation that sights along the line of succession to see a future in which mature leaders maintain the momentum of the movement until the Father's redemptive purpose is fulfilled;

—I leave you an organization unified by the bond of love in Christ, representative of the body of Christ in spirit, and effective as a mediator for the cause of Christ in the culture of our time;

—I leave you the gift of agape or sacrificial love exemplified by my leadership, imitated by my followers, and demonstrated by our organization as our ultimate witness in the world.

The legacies of trust, truth, and love lead in only one direction—to the evidence of greater things giving glory to God the Father and to his Son, Jesus Christ. All other outcomes fade into vaporous ends. To that end, I submit my leadership to the judgment of those who know me best—my superiors in authority, my peers in administration, my subordinates in reporting, and my constituents in support. Your administration will be judged by the same expectations. The gifts I leave to you as my successor now become the debt you owe as a leader. May you and those entrusted to you be *true to his trust, transformed by his truth, and unified by his love.* The gift of greater things awaits you.

Acknowledgments

SUCCESSION IN LEADERSHIP CAN be a bane or a blessing. My wife, Jan, and I experienced both sides in the three transitions during our thirty-three-year career in the presidency of Christian higher education. After writing this book, I applied the Succession Principle to each of these transitions and thought about those whom I succeeded and those who succeeded me. When I saw the whole picture I realized how blessed we are. Those who preceded us stepped aside graciously and gave us their full support. Those who succeeded us always honored us and cared for us. So, it is time to give gratitude to our predecessors in our presidencies—Roderick J. Smith at Spring Arbor Junior College, C. Dorr Demaray at Seattle Pacific College, and Frank Bateman Stanger at Asbury Theological Seminary. On the side of succession are those who succeeded us—Elwood Voller at Spring Arbor College, David LeShana at Seattle Pacific University, and Maxie Dunnam at Asbury Theological Seminary. Colleagues, yes, and friends forever.

Another book needs to be written on succession for spouses in presidential leadership. Whether bane or blessing, transition's impact on them is magnified. In our case, Jan remembers the first ladies who preceded her and whom she succeeded as one of life's special blessings. Ruth Smith at Spring Arbor, Grace Demaray at Seattle Pacific, and Mardelle Stanger at Asbury Seminary preceded her and Beth Avery Voller, Becky LeShana, and Jerry Dunnam succeeded her. To this day, Jan counts each of these women as sisters in a society of mutual understanding and support.

Deepest gratitude goes to Gayle Beebe, president of Westmont College, for writing a foreword that puts undeserved gloss on the author. Thanks as well to friends who read the manuscript and commented on it—Bud Austin, president emeritus of LeTourneau University; Dan Busby, president of the Evangelical Council for Financial Accountability; Jodi Detrick, Women's Ministry Director, Northwest Ministry Network; Maxie Dunnam, president emeritus of Asbury Theological Seminary; Phil Eaton, president emeritus of Seattle Pacific University; David Goodnight, a Seattle attorney; Dan Martin, president of Seattle Pacific University; Steve Moore, executive director of the Murdock Trust; David Le Shana, president emeritus of both Seattle Pacific University and George Fox University; Kimberly Rupert, provost of Spring Arbor University; and Blake Wood, lead pastor of Seattle First Free Methodist Church. Once again, Sheila Lovell, executive assistant to the president during my tenure at Asbury Theological Seminary, saved the day for me by editing and formatting the manuscript. As with succession itself, there are no soloists in the orchestration of this book.

David L. McKenna

Bibliography

60 Minutes. October 9, 2000. CBSNews.com.staff.

The American Heritage Dictionary. New York: Dell, 1982.

Aslan, Reza. *The Zealot: The Life and Times of Jesus of Nazareth.* New York: Aslan Media, 2013.

Bakke, Ray. *A Theology as Big as the City.* Downers Grove, IL: InterVarsity, 1997.

Barker, Joel Arthur. *Future Edge.* New York: William Morrow and Company, 1992.

Batterson, Mark. *All In.* Grand Rapids: Zondervan, 2013.

Bellah, Robert, et al. *Habits of the Heart.* Berkeley, CA: University of California Press, 1981.

Bennis, Warren, and Burt Nanus. *Leaders.* New York: Harper & Row, 1985.

Bornstein, Rita. "Succession Planning: The Time Has Come." *Trusteeship,* September-October, 2010. agb.org/trusteeship/2010/septemberoctober/succession-planning -time-has-come.

Brown, Daniel James. *The Boys in the Boat.* New York: Viking, 2013.

Buford, Bob. *Drucker and Me.* Brentwood, TN: Worthy Publications, 2014.

Campolo, Tony. *It's Friday, Sunday's Comin'.* Nashville: Thomas Nelson, 2008.

"A Christian in Winter—Billy Graham at 75." *Time,* November 15, 1993. Content.time. com/time/magazine/article/0.9171.979573.00.html.

Colson, Charles. *The Body.* Nashville: Thomas Nelson, 1992.

Crouch, Andy. *Playing God: Redeeming the Gift of Power.* Downers Grove, IL: InterVarsity, 2013.

De Pree, Max. *Leadership Is an Art.* New York: Dell, 1989.

Dilbert. Seattle Times, February 27, 2014.

Dostoyevsky, Fyodor. *The Idiot.* New York: Barnes and Noble Classics, 2004.

Emerson, Ralph Waldo. "Thoreau." *The Atlantic Monthly.* www.theatlantic.com/magazine/ archive/1862/08/thoreau/306418/.

Friedman, Michael J. *Free at Last: The U.S. Civil Rights Movement.* Washington, DC: US Department of State, Bureau of International Information Programs, 2008. Photos. state.gov/libraries/korea/49271/dwoa.122709/free_at_last.pdf.

Friedman, Thomas. *The Lexus and the Olive Tree.* New York: First Anchor, 2000.

Gallup Politics. "Honesty and Ethics Rating of Clergy Slides to New Low." December 16, 2013. www.gallup.com/poll/1654/honesty-ethics-professors.aspx.

Gossip, Arthur John. "But When Life Tumbles In, What Then?" In *The Protestant Pulpit: An Anthology of Master Sermons from the Reformation to Our Day,* edited by Andrew Watterson Blackwood, 198–204. Grand Rapids: Baker, 1984.

Gross, Anthony. *Lincoln's Own Stories*. New York: Harper and Brothers, 1912.

"In the Garden." In *The Hymnal of Worship and Celebration*, 425. Irving, TX: Word Music, 1989.

Isaacson, Walter. *Steve Jobs*. New York: Simon and Schuster, 2011.

Kinghorn, Kenneth, ed. *A Celebration of Ministry: Essays in Honor of Frank Bateman Stanger*. Wilmore, KY: Francis Asbury, 1982.

Kolodiejchuk, Brian. *Mother Teresa: Come Be My Light: The Private Writings of the "Saint of Calcutta."* New York: Doubleday, 2007.

Lawrence [Brother]. *The Practice of the Presence of God*. New Kensington, PA: Whitaker House, 2008.

"Leadership Model." Acumen, acumen.org/leaders/.

Lewis, C. S. "Becoming Clean Mirrors." In *C. S. Lewis: Readings for Meditation and Reflection*, edited by Walter Hooper, 39–40. New York: HarperCollins, 1996.

———. "The Efficacy of Prayer." In *The World's Last Night and Other Essays*, 3–11. New York: Houghton Mifflin Harcourt Brace, 2012.

McKenna, David. *Christ-Centered Leadership: The Incarnational Difference*. Eugene, OR: Cascade, 2013.

———. *Power to Follow; Grace to Lead*. Dallas: Word, 1989.

Moffett, Samuel. "What Makes the Korean Church Grow?" *Christianity Today*, January 31, 2007. www.christianitytoday.com/ct/2007/januaryweb-only/105-33.o.html.

Nierenberg, Roger. *Maestro: A Surprising Story about Leading by Listening*. London: Penguin, 2009.

Nouwen, Henri. *In the Name of Jesus*. New York: Crossroad, 1991.

Phillips, J. B., trans. *The New Testament in Modern English*. New York: The MacMillan Company, 1958.

"Pyrrhus of Epirus." Wikipedia. En.wikipedia.org/wiki/Pyrrhus_of_Epirus.

Stott, John. *The Message of 2 Timothy*. Downers Grove, IL: InterVarsity, 1973.

Sweet, Leonard. "The Church in the 21st Century." Address at the Leadership Network Conference, 1994.

Tuchman, Barbara. *The March of Folly: From Troy to Vietnam*. New York: Alfred A. Knopf, 1984.

Taylor, Howard. *Hudson Taylor's Spiritual Secret*. London: China Inland Mission, 1932.

Wiesel, Elie. *Night*. Foreword by Francois Mauriac. New York: Hill and Wang, 2006.

Worthen, Molly. *Apostles of Reason: The Crisis of Authority in American Evangelicalism*. Oxford: Oxford University Press, 2014.

Wuthnow, Robert. *Christianity in the 21st Century*. Oxford: Oxford University Press, 1993.

Yancey, Philip. *The Question that Never Goes Away*. Grand Rapids: Zondervan, 2013.

Made in the USA
Middletown, DE
22 March 2017